DMZ I
VIETNAM

Phil Marshall

*To Slick Rich —
Thanks for all your
help. Great to call
you a friend!
Phil Marshall*

OS Publishing
PO Box 1
Ludlow Falls, Ohio 45339 USA

DMZ DUSTOFF
VIETNAM

Front and back cover photos by:
Ed Iacobacci, Medic

All books are available in Braille, Giant Print, Kindle… Auto-delivered wirelessly and for corporate training, premiums, or special promotions.

For details contact Charles Lee Emerson, Proprietary Markets, OS Publishing, PO Box 1, Ludlow Falls, Ohio 45339 USA.

ISBN 978-1-47830-716-7

Printed in the United States of America.

Contents   Page

Contents cont.   Page

"DMZ Dustoff"

True, First Person Stories Of The Men Who Flew MEDEVAC Missions

In Vietnam

Introduction

This introduction is rather long... If you want to get into the meat of this book right away, go to "Mission 1" and then come back here. Otherwise, read on and thank you for your interest in what we did, oh, so many years ago...

It's common knowledge among the military that the only difference between a "War Story" and a "Fairy Tale" is that a Fairy Tale starts with "Once upon a time..." and a War Story starts with "This is no shit..." That is the only difference between the two. As you will see, not one of these stories starts with "Once upon a time," they are not Fairy Tales.

This book is dedicated to a couple hundred men who flew with the 237th Medical Detachment, Helicopter Ambulance, from 1968 to 1973 in Vietnam. The 237th was the last Dustoff unit to arrive in Vietnam and the last to leave.

Affectionately called "DMZ Dustoff" by the men who flew these missions of rescue, rather than just "Dustoff," they were all volunteers and could have quit flying the missions at any time... But they didn't. In fact, several men already in country and not initially assigned to Dustoff volunteered to fly these Medevac missions, knowing the dangers.

Some sources claim that a Dustoff crew was over 3 times more likely to be a casualty than other types of helicopter missions. We were proud of the fact that we were the northern-most Dustoff unit in South Vietnam and also proud of our accomplishments. Flying these missions was incredibly dangerous but it was also incredibly rewarding, unlike anything most of us have ever experienced since, and most likely never will again.

After the war, it was determined that 98% of the wounded that were picked up in our Huey helicopters with the red crosses painted on them survived the war. If they were breathing when we got to them, they most likely would survive, 98 times out of 100. The Wall in Washington DC would have been much larger had it not been for all these men and their helicopters, not to mention the Medical teams who took care of the wounded after we delivered them.

But this "success" rate did not come cheaply. DMZ Dustoff lost 15 brave men in service to their country, their fellow soldiers, and to the people of Vietnam. An unofficial count by this author shows at least 8 of our UH-1H Huey aircraft were destroyed and several more were heavily damaged. Many other aircraft suffered serious damage and were either returned to the States for major overhaul or were left in country for the South Vietnamese Air Force when our troops came home. Virtually every helicopter that flew in the 237th had battle scars to display its combat record.

Collecting these stories has been an adventure in itself. It has taken several years. At first, some did not want to talk about their missions. "I don't remember" was sometimes offered, but then, later, it became "I remember but I don't *want* to remember." Eventually, even those stories came out. Others were more open about their experiences but without exception they always praised everyone else in the crew rather than themselves. Sometimes it was tears, sometimes it was laughter, but it was always with respect. Respect for each other and respect for the patients.

The Army says that all totaled, Dustoff units carried almost 1 million patients during the war; that means that about 1 in 2.5 at some time or another got a flight in a Huey with the Red Cross. Maybe they were wounded, maybe they were sick, and maybe they just needed to be transferred to another hospital... They all got to fly in the Medevac Hueys. The men in combat in the field knew that if they had need, the Dustoff crews would be there as soon as possible to take them out of harm's way. Quite often, within minutes of being wounded, they were being treated in a hospital.

Normally, we would fly with only a half tank of fuel. Because weight is critical in a helicopter, flying with 700 pounds less fuel meant we could haul out 3 or 4 more wounded on the first trip if necessary. If things were that bad, if there were a lot of casualties, we certainly did not want to go back a second time unless we had to! For that reason, the 237th and most other Dustoff units, did not carry mounted machine guns with ammunition, either. Again, not only would the additional weight affect our ability to carry wounded, we believed our Crew Chief and Medic were better utilized attending to the patients than they would be firing weapons at targets they probably couldn't even see.

On one of my last night missions, we picked up 15 wounded South Vietnamese soldiers. With mounted weapons, ammo and a full tank of fuel, we would never have got the helicopter off the ground.

It must be noted here that in our understanding of the Geneva Conventions, Medical Ambulances and their crews were permitted to carry weapons to protect their patients only, not for offensive use. In addition, these same ambulances were not permitted to carry "resupply ammo" or offensive troops, either; they were to be used only as Medical transports. However, it was common practice for the enemy to shoot at these unarmed helicopters with the very prominent red crosses and many men were killed and many helicopters were lost because of this disregard for the Medical markings. What is ironic is that many times American lives were risked to provide Medical treatment and quick extraction by helicopter to these same enemy soldiers, yet they continued to shoot at the red crosses.

It was also our understanding that the enemy soldier who shot down ANY American helicopter was awarded a medal and was given a sum equal to about $500 USD, approximately a year's pay for them.

I would think that the money was sent to the family of the soldier, as what good is 500 bucks in the jungle?

Regarding the actual rescues, our "method of operation" was to get there in a hurry, make the pick-up in a hurry and get out in a hurry. Every second on the ground could be critical. Very rarely did we wait for gunship cover. If the guns were already there, great, but we knew time was critical and we wasted not a minute. Going into a Landing Zone (LZ) fast and usually at a very low altitude or even tree top level, generally gave us the element of surprise and cover that we needed to survive. Huey helicopters are loud but incredibly reliable and allowed us to maneuver them in configurations that were probably never considered by the Bell Helicopter Company, manufacturer of these incredible machines. Thank you, Bell, for giving us such an amazing aircraft!

For the most part, when we returned home from the War, we experienced apathy. Some claim outward hostility was shown to them, but no one spit on me and no one called me a baby killer; it was just apathy. We, as Vietnam Veterans, have made a conscious, or perhaps even unconscious, effort to make sure that it never happens to our troops again.

Pilot and crew humor can be quite strange and macabre; it was how we survived the stress of the sometimes harrowing missions and being away from family and friends at home. Someone wasn't killed in action, they "Bought the Farm," apparently a nicer way of saying someone died. Or quite often, as we were racing to a helicopter for an urgent mission, it was not unusual to hear someone yell out, "If you don't make it back, can I have your fan?" Fans were a very valuable commodity as they were usually in short supply in this hot, humid climate. It was our way of telling each other to be careful and fly safe… Kinda like "Break a leg" in the theater, I suppose. Good friends can sometimes be hard to find, but not while we were flying in Vietnam; they were all around.

I have tried to explain the gamut of emotions in these stories because our feelings ran the entire continuum; from good to bad, from serious to not serious, from adrenaline highs to lows. But we were *always* dedicated to the mission. For our tour in Vietnam, we used each other for support; we were friends, family and confidants to each other, all rolled into one. But more than that, the flight crews absolutely depended on each other for their lives.

The pilots depended on the Crew Chief and Medic; the guys in the back depended on the pilots up front. To the man, I am so proud to have served with Dustoff and even more proud of *all* the men of the 237th. They performed at their best on a daily basis; they are my brothers. And we were very young!

Generally, the crewmembers in the back were around 18 to 20 years old. Because Flight School required about 9 months of training, the pilots were generally a year older, 19 to 21 or 22. A few were even 23 or 24! One of my favorite stories on this subject was Warrant Officer David "GoGo" Gomez, one of my best buds in country. The Army's Warrant Officer Flight School did not require a college education or degree, only a High School diploma. Because of this, many guys enlisted for helicopter training right out of high school when they were still 18 years of age. A year later, they would then be in Vietnam with wings on their chests and bars on their collars... WO1, Warrant Officer 1, or lovingly referred to as "Wobbly Ones."

As an Officer, Gomez was appointed to be our unit's Voting Officer as one of his additional duties. However, 2 months later, it was realized that he was not old enough to vote yet!

Having enlisted right out of High School, he was now flying in combat at the age of 19, yet he wasn't old enough to vote nor could he even legally buy alcohol back in the States. At that time, one had to be 21. Reminded of this military "faux pas" years later, Gomez told me, "If I'm not mistaken, I was still 19 when I was made an Aircraft Commander." Incredible... Can't vote, can't drink, but he can command a helicopter, the crew and the single ship missions in a hostile combat zone. Way to go, Uncle Sam!

Many Vietnam Veteran helicopter pilots have opined over the years that old men make wars and young men fight them. We were expendable then, and so were our aircraft. Guys were lining up to attend flight school and thousands of helicopters were sent to Vietnam; over 4000 aircraft were lost during the war. If a pilot survived an aircraft loss, it was, "No problem, here's another helicopter, try to be more careful this time!"

And, of course, along with the youthful exuberance of all the flight crews came a certain bravado and brashness.

Occasionally, a pilot or crewman might do something "questionable" and when someone would bring it to their attention, the most common reply would usually be something like, "What are they gonna do, send me to Vietnam?"

The Dustoff stories included here are not all that there are, there are many more that will probably never be put to paper or even told. Maybe because the storyteller is no longer with us or because those involved are no longer in touch with us; they have faded into the masses, never to speak out loud of their dreams or nightmares. But one thing remains a fact, all of these stories are absolutely true and as close to the actual events as I can possibly make them. They all happened just as you will read about them and they are not embellished. In fact, some of the material, I felt, could have been "sanitized" but if I did that, the reader would not fully appreciate what we had to deal with. So while I tried to keep the narratives from becoming *too* graphic, I couldn't do much without affecting the authenticity of the story.

The only thing I can't do for you is reproduce the sound of a Huey gas turbine engine spooling up at start or the distinctive sound of a Huey's rotor blades rushing to a rescue. I can't reproduce the smells of spent gunpowder, the smells of fresh blood on a wounded soldier, the smells of the burning jet fuel or the smells of a body bag as it's loaded onto the cold, hard floor of our helicopters. Trust me, once you experience those sounds and those "fragrances" you will never forget them and anything closely resembling them will instantly take a Vietnam Veteran back to a land far, far away. A far away land, but *never* far enough from memory.

To emphasize how powerful these sensory inputs can be to a Vietnam Vet, I offer this brief "anecdote." At a recent reunion of 237th crews, a crewmember that shall remain nameless here was offered a flight on the Huey that was also present. He declined, saying only, "After 18 months of flying in country, I only want to hear it start one more time; I want to hear the igniters clicking and the sound of the engine spooling up, the smell of the fuel. I don't need to fly again" as his voice trailed off to a whisper.

He stood nearby as the aircraft was fired up, and probably with eyes closed, he did indeed, once again, experience those all too familiar sounds and smells... And he promptly wet his pants. Nothing major, only a small stain, but no one who noticed said a word; it wasn't necessary. They each understood the emotional attachment many of these men have to the Huey and the missions we flew together.

Within a year, this crewmember passed away, but he got one last visit with his youth, one last visit to the times when he tried to make a difference in the world, one rescue at a time.

To illustrate our missions, I have a resource of over 2,300 photos (and growing as I find new crewmembers) of the 237th to choose from and have tried to use the best ones available. However, there are many more excellent photos that could have been used, they were all contributed by 237th members to form an archive of our time in country. These photos, along with digitally copied rolls of 8mm movies taken by us, will be donated to the Smithsonian Institution and should be available to anyone who cares to see them.

Please study the photos in this book carefully to note the details of our missions and our equipment, it was how we lived.

The 2-piece Nomex uniforms that we wore were developed specifically for aircrews during the Vietnam War. They worked so well that these "fire suits" were soon adapted by NASCAR, USAC, the NHRA and other competition organizations. Somewhat improved, I'm sure; they are still in use today.

Only days before publication of this book, a friend forwarded the following to me via email. While I cannot verify the authenticity of it, I thought it very well describes what we were doing as pilots in Vietnam. The email read:

Not widely known is the fact that in 1966-67, a year before his death, John Steinbeck, Nobel and Pulitzer Prize winner, went to Vietnam at the request of his friend Harry F. Guggenheim, publisher of Newsday, to do a series of reports on the war. The reports took the form of letters to his dear friend Alicia Patterson, Newsday's first editor and publisher. Those letters have been published in a book by Thomas E. Barden, Vietnam veteran and professor of English at the University of Toledo.

The book is entitled, "Steinbeck on Vietnam: Dispatches From The War."

Alicia, I wish I could tell you about these pilots. They make me sick with envy. They ride their vehicles the way a man controls a fine, well-trained quarter horse. They weave along streambeds, rise like swallows to clear trees, they turn and twist and dip like swifts in the evening. I watch their hands and feet on the controls; the delicacy of the coordination reminds me of the sure and seeming slow hands of (Pablo) Casals on the cello. They are truly musicians' hands and they play their controls like music and they dance them like ballerinas and they make me jealous because I want so much to do it. Remember your child night dream of perfect flight free and won-derful? It's like that, and sadly I know I never can. My hands are too old and forgetful to take orders from the command center, which speaks of updrafts and side winds, of drift and shift, or ground fire indicated by a tiny puff or flash, or a hit and all these commands must be obeyed by the musicians hands instantly and automatically. I must take my longing out in admiration and the joy of seeing it. Sorry about that leak of ecstasy, Alicia, but I had to get it out or burst."

In 1969, each crew averaged about 75 patients a month and about 75 hours a month; the 75 patients a month were field pickups, not patient transfers. "Each crew" meaning the two pilots, crew chiefs and medics on each aircraft. While other crews such as gunships, slicks (troop transports) and scout helicopters probably flew twice as many hours as we did, we probably flew two or three times more takeoffs and landings due to the nature of our missions. I'm not saying that made us better pilots, I'm only saying that we had a lot more take offs and landings per hour of flight time. A typical mission for us could easily be 3 or 4 takeoffs and landings and may only last 30 to 45 mins.

I would also like to recognize Specialist Richard Villa, one of the finest Crew Chiefs I have ever flown with. "Pancho" as he was obviously called, was not only a dedicated Dustoff crewmember he has also been a great partner in putting together our DMZ Dustoff reunions. We share many missions and many stories together. After we finally reconnected after many years, he asked me if I thought others would be interested in getting together, so we gave it a shot. It seems that many others were interested and we have had some wonderful times getting together again.

Any profit from the sale of these books goes to help defray the costs of future reunions; I have no desire to profit from these books myself. Thanks, Pancho!

Richard "Pancho" Villa, right, and Ted Issacson, working on a Huey engine cover.

In writing these stories, I am certain that I have made some punctuation and grammatical mistakes. My apologies to my favorite High School English teacher, Jane Rice, but in trying to keep costs down, I have edited this myself.

Please just enjoy the stories as they are written and don't get hung up on the minutia.

Finally, while a word or two in these stories may not be *exactly* as originally spoken due to 40 years of memory, I have tried my best to sort out the details with those memories that are sometimes conflicting. It is my hope you will come away with an appreciation of what Dustoff units, especially the 237th, accomplished in combat. With apologies, also, to those who find the occasional four-letter word in these stories to be offensive, I reiterate to the reader that these are not fairy tales; these are "No shit!"

Warrant Officer Phil Marshall
DMZ Dustoff 7-1-1
Camp Evans and Quang Tri
Vietnam, 1969

The Author at an American Huey 369 Event.
Photo By Kae York

About The Author

R. Phillip Marshall received his first helicopter flight at the age of 16. His cousin, Larry Mason, flew the first helicopter for Channel 9 Television News in Cincinnati, Ohio. Phil was immediately hooked on flying, but had no idea that he, too, might someday become a helicopter pilot.

Graduating in 1966 from Beavercreek High School near Dayton, Ohio, Phil went on to Ohio State University to become a teacher. But as he readily admits, "I was too concerned about where the parties were and not concerned enough about where the Library was!"

With too many "Cs" and "Ds" and not enough "As" and "Bs," he did not have the Grade Point Average to return to Ohio State the next year. "I went to a nearby Junior College for a couple of semesters but I knew that if I was not going full time to a 4 year University or if I wasn't married with at least one child, I was probably going to be drafted."

With this in mind, he started visiting Recruiters, stopping at the Army first. As soon as Warrant Officer Flight School was mentioned, the recruiter had Phil's full attention; he would train to be a helicopter pilot!

Basic Training began in April of 1968 and graduation from Rotary Wing Flight School was in April of 1969. Having been selected to fly Dustoff before completion of flight school, Phil attended what was referred to as a "condensed Combat Medic's Course" at Ft. Sam Houston, San Antonio, Texas. There, 24 pilots from Phil's flight class of over 200 men received the 10-week Combat Medic Course in 5-weeks.

He arrived in Vietnam on the 4th of July 1969, and was assigned to the 237th Medical Detachment, Helicopter Ambulance, at Camp Evans in Northern I Corps; they were the northernmost Dustoff unit in Vietnam.

He was given the call sign "Dustoff 7-1-1." "I wasn't superstitious," he stated, "but I never said 'seven-eleven', it was always seven-one-one." With most of the Aircraft Commanders in the 237th going home at the end of November, Phil was made an Aircraft Commander on 11 November 1969, after only 3 months of flying in combat. On 15 November, just 4 days later, he was wounded on a night rescue mission and subsequently sent back to the States due to the nature of his wound.

Further assignment was to Ft. Wolters, Texas, home of Primary Flight Training, where Phil volunteered to be a Training, Advising and Counseling (TAC) Officer for new Warrant Officer Candidates.

He remained in this capacity until his Honorable Discharge in April of 1971.

Most recently, he has become involved with American Huey 369, in Peru, Indiana, which is a group of veterans and patriots who have restored Huey helicopters to flying condition for the preservation, demonstration and education of the Huey. The AH369 organization pays tribute to *all* veterans and patriots, but especially Vietnam Veterans.

These restored Vietnam Veteran Hueys appear at many events in Indiana and surrounding states several times a year.

This organization can be found on the Internet at:

AmericanHuey369.com

Photo Contributors
Officers

Chris Bannigan
Michael Bradley Family
Joe Brown Family
Ann Cunningham
Joel Dozhier
Maryanna Dube Hiester
Dave "Go-Go" Gomez
Dave Hansen
Bob Hill Family
"Slick" Rick Marotte
Phil Marshall
Erich Menger
Dean Pedings Family
Sandy Petersen
Thomas Robby Robinson
Phil Roby
George Rose Yakush
Diana Sebek
Phillip Schmitz Family

Quincy Sittingdown
Dave Tousignant
Lee Wood
George and (Vietnam Nurse) Carol Zuvela

Photo Contributors <u>Enlisted Men</u>

Allen Covey Family
Dan DeSande
Dan "The Nose" Fanelli
Clem Grillo
Wayne Doc Gordie Gordon
Dan "Doc" Halliday
David Reeves
Ed Harpt
Ed Iacobacci
Ted Isaacson
Al "Jinx" Jenkins
Tommy Johnson
John Largent Family
Tony Lopez
Randy Love Family
David MacLurg Family
John Moore
Geoff Morris
Richard Mullen
Kim Peters
Richard Villa
Charlie Whaley
Jeff White Family
Ellis Woodcock

This Book Is Dedicated

To my parents, Lois and "Whitey" Marshall, who always encouraged and supported me in whatever I did.

To my sisters Janice and Jeannette, who showed much pride in what their little brother was doing, even when supporting the troops in Vietnam was not popular. Many "CARE" packages as we called them, arrived from home almost weekly and were most appreciated. While the homemade chocolate chip cookies usually arrived as a box of crumbs, I knew they were baked with love and thoughts of seeing me home again.

Thanks to my wife Teresa for her patience with me while I put this book together.

This is also dedicated to my best friend in High School LCpl. John W. Stahl who was killed in action in Vietnam on 26 September 1968.

Thanks to my High School classmate and fellow Vietnam Aircraft Commander and Helicopter Pilot Charles Lee Emerson for helping me put this in print.

Honor Roll

This Book Is Also Dedicated To...
The Men Of The 237TH
Who Were "KIA," Killed In Action
They Gave Their Lives
So That Others May Live

May 22, 1969

Sp5 David J. Ewing, Medic
KIA while serving with the
54th Medical Detachment
(Original 237th Member)

April 27, 1970

CPT. John R. Hill, Aircraft Commander
SP4 Zettie J. C. Dulin, Crewchief
PFC Randall W. Love, Medic

May 10, 1970

WO1 Alfred J. Gaidis, Aircraft Commander
1LT Phillip N. Schmitz, Pilot
SP4 John Alyn Largent, Crewchief
SP4 Charles Allen Covey, Medic

September 27, 1970

SP4 David W. MacLurg, Medic

September 27, 1970

CW2 Robert Hill, Aircraft Commander
WO1 Michael Lee Bradley, Pilot
SP4 Jeffery M. White, Crew Chief
SP5 Kenneth C. Nokes, Medic

February 18, 1971

CW2 Joseph G. Brown, Aircraft Commander

June 15, 1971

CW2 Billy Dean Pedings, Aircraft Commander
SP5 Donald Wood, Medic

The History of the 237th can be found on our website:

DmzDustoff.org

How They Died

The 237th Medical Detachment, Helicopter Ambulance, lost 15 pilots and crewmembers; 8 to accidents and 7 to hostile fire, 7 pilots and 8 "guys in the back." This was typical of helicopter operations in Vietnam where approximately half of all losses were due to accident and half to the enemy. (All of our accidental losses in DMZ Dustoff were at night during bad weather.) There are over 2,200 helicopter pilots listed on The Wall in Washington, D.C. with virtually the same number of crewmen. Thus, our losses in DMZ Dustoff were "typical."

I also tried to determine how many of our 237th crewmembers were wounded or injured. While several were accounted for in an informal survey, I knew of many others that were not included in the final tally. Suffice it to say that at LEAST 15 were wounded or injured, perhaps 20 to 25, but I can guess no closer than that.

While I am providing some details of our losses so that the reader might appreciate what we went through, some details have been omitted to protect the families.

As for myself and those that I discussed it with, our biggest fear in flying these missions was that of a post-crash fire. Our next biggest fear was surviving a crash and being captured. Our third biggest fear was not going home alive, but that was never really talked about.

Following is a brief synopsis of each of our DMZ Dustoff losses:

Captain John R. Hill
Pilot & Commanding Officer of the 237th
Specialist 4 Zettie (Zeb) J. C. Dulin
Crew Chief
Private First Class Randy W. Love
Medic
Aircraft 67-17626

On April 27th, 1970, the decision was made to return to DMZ Dustoff at Quang Tri from Da Nang, about an hour's flight away. Departure was made even though it was rather late at night and weather was closing in. Aircrews have a term for this; it's called "get-home-itis," which comes from an overwhelming desire to get "home" at almost any cost and was probably a factor in this loss.

Flights were very "loose" in Vietnam. When away from your home base, there was no flight following required nor was any flight planning necessary; no paperwork at all. One just fired up the aircraft, asked the tower for permission to take off and flew wherever, anytime. No questions asked. That was the situation on this night.

While flying north over Da Nang Harbor, the cloud layer was dropping, and not wanting to climb through the clouds and fly under Instrument Flight Rules (IFR); they decided to descend to lower altitudes, staying under the clouds. A heading was taken to fly around a peninsula at the northern end of the harbor called the Alpha Uniform but as they neared the point, they realized that they were now very close to the water, having continued losing altitude to stay out of the clouds. The pilots attempted a 180-degree turn to return to Da Nang when Zeb called out "Water!"

It was at this point that the aircraft or rotor blades struck the water and sank. Zeb and the Co-Pilot were able to escape the aircraft, as did Captain Hill, who unfortunately had a broken or severely injured arm. Randy Love was not seen on the surface at any time. Hill became separated from Zeb and the Co-Pilot, who then also became separated.

The Co-Pilot was eventually able to find some floating debris and was found the next morning by a routine South Vietnamese patrol boat. He had chanced upon a buoy in the harbor and that was where he was found, still alive, hanging onto the buoy. Dulin and Love's bodies were eventually recovered while Hill's was not. John R. Hill is still listed as KIA, BNR; Killed In Action, Body Not Recovered.

**Captain John R. Hill, 237th Commanding Officer
And Pilot**

Crew Chief Zettie "Zeb" Dulin

Medic Randy Love

Because we did a lot of flying over water due to our missions to the USS Sanctuary and USS Repose, Navy hospital ships, we were issued water wings. I doubt few, if anyone, had tried to put them on, at least no one that I know of, including myself. As pilots, we simply draped them over the backs of our seats with our M16 rifles; I have no idea where the guys in the back kept theirs. We all knew for a fact that in an emergency exit from the helicopter, if something were not attached to us, it would be left in the aircraft. Again, no one, including me, wore them over the water; we just kept them "nearby." It appears here, that is exactly what happened in this accident; no one exited with their wings.

10 May 1970
WO1 Alfred J. Gaidis
Aircraft Commander
1LT Phillip N. Schmitz, Co-Pilot
SP4 John Alyn Largent, Crew Chief
SP4 Charles Allen Covey, Medic
A/C 67-17673

Al Gaidis was a relatively new, but fully qualified, Aircraft Commander; Phillip Schmitz had only been in country a week or so at the time of this loss.

In fact, when Schmitz first arrived in the unit, there was a shortage of Co-Pilots and he was immediately put in a Huey before he had a chance to even empty out his duffel bag! "Grab your flight suit, LT, you're going flying!" Or words to that effect.

The rescue mission was on Dong Ha Mountain. A normal approach to the LZ at the top of the peak was attempted and they received heavy fire. Gaidis broke off the attempt, flew away from the area and dropped down to treetop level. Screaming along the ground at 120 knots, he did a cyclic climb up the side of the mountain and again received heavy fire, only this time from more than one position and with large caliber weapons. Again, they broke off the approach, but this time the aircraft was mortally wounded. A trailing Cobra gunship, call sign "Griffin," called to them on the radio and told them, "You're on fire and losing fuel. You need to put it down now!" A radio call came back, "I think I can make it to the river."

It was about this point that the aircraft went inverted and crashed into the ground, still on fire. A post crash investigation determined that Gaidis had been wounded before the helicopter crashed.

This was evidenced by the fact that the Medic, Covey, had his gloves off and had been attempting first aid on the injured pilot when they crashed. Also, the pilot's seat had been pivoted back to allow the Medic access to the injured pilot. As an ironic end to this crash, according to Army records, a 5th soldier, PFC James Arthur Blackmon, was also killed when the helicopter crashed. He was from the 101st Airborne Division.

Official records show the 5th KIA as a passenger; however, my interviews with those in the 237th at the time of the crash all agree that there was no one else in the helicopter. This 5th unfortunate soul was simply in the wrong place at the wrong time as the aircraft apparently crashed on top of him. There were other US soldiers on the ground in the area of the crash, working their way down the mountain.

Warrant Officer Al Gaidis, Aircraft Commander

1LT Phillip Schmitz, Co-Pilot

Specialist John Largent, Crew Chief

Charles A. Covey, Medic
Covey was originally a "ground Medic" with the 5th Mechanized Division, but wanted to fly. He volunteered to transfer to DMZ Dustoff.

27 Sept 1970
Aircraft 69-15297:
SP4 David W. MacLurg, Medic
Aircraft 69-15021:
CW2 Robert O. Hill, Aircraft Commander
WO1 Michael Lee Bradley, Pilot
SP4 Jeffery M. White, Crew Chief
SP5 Kenneth C. Nokes, Medic

On this night of infamy, 5 brave men lost their lives for the rescue of a Vietnamese child who was badly burned, but that was the nature of our business... So others might live. AC Walt Adams, Co-Pilot Joel Dozhier and Medic David MacLurg (Crew Chief unknown) were called out on this foul-weather night because the child had pulled a boiling pot of water onto himself, causing severe burns over 85% of his body. The rescue was made, the child dropped off at the hospital, and the crew was returning to base when the aircraft suffered a flight instrument failure. The failure of the instruments critical to flight in bad weather caused the crew to have a hard landing, breaking Adam's back and breaking MacLurg's neck, causing his death. Although the aircraft rolled onto it's side during the crash, the Co-Pilot and Crew Chief were not seriously injured and there was no post crash fire.

Two crews were launched to try to locate the downed Huey as no word was heard from them. Steve Woods, a 571st pilot and probably the most experienced IFR pilot in either the 237th or the 571st decided that it was too dangerous and after about 15 minutes or so of searching returned to base.

However, Bob Hill pressed on into the storm in search of his friends. Before long, there were no answers to radio calls to Hill and it was then assumed that he, too, was down. Whether he had crashed or not was a matter of conjecture at the time, but Commanding Officers correctly determined that no more search aircraft would be sent out until morning.

Crew Chief Kim Peters picks up the story from here:

"By late August 1970, Hal Stone and I had been in country going on 18 months and we were short and counting. About the same time, we put ourselves in for replacement as Crew Chiefs. I got my replacement in early September and after about a week of training him, I was relieved of my ship and duties as a Crew Chief and became part of the general maintenance crew again. Then I just sat back and did what all-good GI's do - party, try to forget and wait.

There were a bunch of us partying the night of September 27, 1970 in our hooch (mine, Hal Stone and Bob Campbell) in Phu Bai (just south of Hue) where we had moved our billeting from Quang Tri in mid-summer of

1970. At this time, Hal Stone had also requested to be replaced as a Crew Chief.

To give you a better idea of the kind of relationships we had in a unit like ours, the attendees to this impromptu gathering included ranking Non-Commissioned Officers, Warrant Officers and some Commissioned Officers. It was an extremely stormy night featuring the prelude to the monsoon season coming and hard to keep the bar-b-que going. We joked all evening about how we were sure happy we didn't have to fly in those conditions and commenting on our "poor buddies" up north who might have to. It was later in the evening, around midnight, when a messenger from the CP (Command Post) came and advised us all that our two birds up at Quang Tri, first and second up, were both missing. The message from our Commanding Officer was to knock it off for the night and get some rest because we were all going on a search and rescue hunt at first daylight.

Early in the AM, 4 ships were getting prepared to fly north, two to replace the downed birds and the other two to begin a search and rescue operation on the two that were missing. There were hopes that there might be some survivors and that it was just a matter of no radio communication.

The missing first up bird was my old bird that I had just given up a few weeks earlier. Although we were no longer flying, Hal Stone and I volunteered to go along as an extra set of eyes and our Commanding Officer took us on board the ship he was piloting out of the 571st – our sister unit.

The day was overcast with a low ceiling and with a few light showers. The moods were pretty somber. We had already been informed that our first missing bird from the night before (my old bird) had been located and had three survivors out of our crew of four. We flew to the location, about a mile or so inland from Highway 1, to check it out and maybe get an idea of the area our second up bird might be found. As I was told at the time, the ship had crashed due to mechanical problems and perhaps partly due to the weather conditions. It was a wreck. I was amazed to think that there were any survivors at all. As I recall the Crew Chief had been injured with a broken back, I think one of the pilots had a compound fractured leg and the other pilot was just banged up a lot. The Medic, David MacLurg, was dead with a broken neck. David was from Auburn, WA, and I was from Seattle, so we had always had a little bit of a bond.

They had responded the night before to a call for a Vietnamese civilian child who had been scalded with boiling water over 85% of his body.

Since we had initially followed Highway 1 north toward Quang Tri, we left that site and began a circling search pattern covering both sides of Highway 1 and a few miles to both the north and south of the initial crash site. We were flying along over Highway 1 when I pointed out to the assigned Crew Chief on board (as extra people on board, Hal and I were not hooked up with their radio communication) at an area of smoke next to the highway that looked suspicious to me. Keep in mind that when you flew over Vietnam, there was smoke constantly everywhere resulting from artillery fire damage and/or its origination, agricultural clearing, cooking fires, just plain war damage, etc.

I thought that this source of smoke was a bit too close to the highway and a bit isolated and didn't make much sense. Our Commanding Officer, who was our Aircraft Commander that day, took us down for a closer look. As we got closer it became apparent that what we were looking at was the burned out remains of a Huey.

We set down about a hundred feet away and I got out to conduct a closer investigation while the crew kept the bird running and ready to go. At this time we didn't know if they had crashed or been shot down. I knew the crew of this downed bird well.

As I got closer I could see the Medic, Ken Nokes, lying just outside the helicopter face down. I signaled back to our bird that I had identified one KIA. Then I walked around to the nose of the aircraft and looked into the burned out shell where two pilots still sat strapped in their seats, Bob Hill and Mike Bradley. I signaled back two more KIA's. Then I checked the rest of the bird for Jeff White, the Crew Chief, but could not find him. I re-checked the aircraft again, and then started searching in an outward circle. I found him lying face down about 50' out in front of the aircraft. He had evidently been thrown that far in the crash. This made KIA number four. They had gone into the air on a night that nobody should have been flying, in an attempt to help and support a crew of their own who were missing. I assumed that they were flying low level looking for our first crew and it appeared that they had literally flown into the ground.

So in one night, trying to help one Vietnamese child, we had lost two birds, had 5 crewmembers killed with two severely injured and none of them from enemy action.

Crew Chief Jeff White's position on the ground and other evidence showed that he had tried to crawl back to the aircraft to assist the rest of the crew, but he succumbed to his injuries, making it no closer to the wreck than 50 feet away. The last sentence in Kim's narrative pretty well sums it up.

Medic David MacLurg

Warrant Officer Bob Hill, Aircraft Commander

Warrant Officer Mike Bradley, Co-Pilot

Crew Chief Specialist Jeff White

Specialist Ken Nokes, Medic

Regarding Ken Nokes, he was another who volunteered to fly Dustoff. His good friend and fellow Medic Ted Sexauer had this to offer:

"We'd made plans to go to school together; we both made 6-month extensions in order to beat the 5-month early out. Might as well tell you the story here. More background, he came to us from the 85th Evacuation Hospital at Phu Bai, and he did the radios for a long time before he started flying. We both had the same amount of time left in enlistment; I extended for the 173d and he extended to fly. It was impossible to stay in touch, but we did pull a lot of strings to be able to go on R&R together, starting October 7. Australia. I was at the R&R center in Da Nang when I learned of his death. He didn't show, and so I called the 571st and got the news. I couldn't believe it. I had to call them back and hear it again. I just didn't think that was in the cards. We had 'til mid-November to ETS, he was a month and a half from safeness."

18 February 1971
CW2 Joseph G. Brown

Warrant Officer Joe Brown spent his first tour as a Cobra Pilot, but wanted to fly Dustoff for his second tour. Thus, he found himself flying DMZ Dustoff helicopters during Lam Son 719. The details of Brown's death when his helicopter was shot down are found in Mission 15 of this book.

Warrant Officer Joe Brown

15 June 1971
CW2 Billy Dean Pedings
SP5 Donald Wood

Warrant Officer Billy Dean Pedings, Pilot, and Specialist Donald Wood, Medic, were also KIA during Lam Son 719, on the same mission when their helicopter was shot down. Their loss is described in Mission 16 of this book.

Warrant Officer Dean Pedings, Pilot

Specialist Donald Wood, Medic With the hoist.

Mission 1

Day The Medic Shot The Bad Guys
1 April 1970
April Fools Day

Somewhere north of QL9, the east-west road through Dong Ha to Laos. North of the artillery firebases such as Alpha 4 and Bravo 1, not that far from the DMZ, Demilitarized Zone, separating North and South Vietnam. Call sign "DMZ Dustoff 707," Aircraft Commander 1LT Gary L. Brink, Co-Pilot Warrant Officer 1 Robin (Rob) Halvorson, Crew Chief Specialist 4 Tommy Johnson and Medic Specialist 5 Frank E. Crockett are on a mission to evacuate wounded in UH-1H 67-17627, one of the original Huey helicopters that deployed overseas with the 237th Medical Detachment in November of 1968.

Brink remembers, "We had an early afternoon mission to pick up a wounded infantryman but we kept getting shot at; we tried a couple of times to get in, but there was just too much incoming." But Halvorson thought he saw a way to get in on his right side of the aircraft so he asked for the controls.

Gary Brink, right, age 24, receiving the Air Medal with "V" Device for Valor on a different mission.

Co-Pilot Rob Halvorson, 19 years old

Approaching at treetop level and high speed, Rob had spotted a draw, or depression in the ground, that he thought he could use to their advantage. Settling into the low spot, Rob remembers, "We were sitting on the ground with the blades maybe only a foot off the ground at the tips, but it gave us the protection we needed and we got the wounded on board. After we lifted out and were pretty much at altitude, what appeared to be a rocket of some sort whizzed straight across the nose of the aircraft, one side to the other. It's almost as if it went by in slow motion" but, of course, it was at "full speed." (This author has been told by more than one Vietnam helicopter pilot that they observed the enemy take aim at their heads, and even though the aircraft was sitting on the ground with no movement other than the blades turning, the enemy would then aim in front of the aircraft and finally pull the trigger. Apparently, these young enemy soldiers were taught to take a bead on the pilot, then lead the aircraft before firing. However, it seems that it was never explained to them that they should fire in front of the aircraft only when it was flying, not stationery on the ground!)

Brink and Halvorson were able to depart the area with no further enemy fire and were on their way to the hospital with their patient when a call came on "Guard." The UHF, Ultra High Frequency, radio has a position for transmitting and receiving "on Guard." When the UHF selector is turned to Guard, a crew can make a radio call and every aircraft within many, many miles of that radio hears the transmission, unless they have specifically disabled Guard reception. As Dustoff crews, we always had the selector on "Guard Receive" as we never knew when an emergency call would come in.

Of course, being young and stupid, full of urine and vinegar helicopter pilots, occasionally one would hear a transmission such as "This is God on Guard, the 1st Cav sucks!" Of course, not to be outdone, a crew might then hear a reply such as "God on Guard, say again, you were cut out by a Mayday.'"

The emergency call on Guard was from a Long Range Reconnaissance Patrol, LRRP team that was in trouble. Brink answered with his DMZ Dustoff 7-oh-7 call sign... The reply was, "Hey Dustoff, we've got a mission for you!" "Where are you?" was Brink's question. "Can't tell you... Where are YOU at?"

You can't tell me? Brink is thinking how do I know which way to go?

He replies to the LRRPs, "I'm just north of the firebases" was Brink's reply. "How are we going to find you?" "Just head North!" Uh, oh; 7-0-7 was already only a couple of klicks (kilometers) away from the DMZ and they want him to go closer! So they head north and before long, they cross the river in the middle of the "Z." "I just crossed a river" with both parties knowing full well "which" river he was referring to. "Just keep coming north." The crew of Dustoff 7-oh-7 was now in North Vietnam.

As they neared the pickup site, another call to the LRRPs (pronounced "lurps") sent a proverbial chill down the spines of the Dustoff crew. The LRRPS were now whispering on the radio, a sure sign that the bad guys were very close! "What are your casualties and have you received recent hostile fire? From what direction?" Typical need-to-know questions asked on virtually every mission to the guys on the ground. "One casualty at this time" and "We hear voices about 20 meters to the north" was another whispered reply.

Twenty meters??? Wait a minute, that's roughly the length of a Huey, and that's how close the enemy is??? And we are supposed to come in, land and load them, all without "disturbing" the bad guys??? No way!

The LRRPS would not pop a smoke grenade to mark their position, but they said they would flash a mirror or lay out a red panel to mark the LZ. Finally locating the red panel in a small field of tall elephant grass, the attempt to land, as always, was made, and here is what happened:

Brink spotted the ground guide. Usually the guys on the ground would stand with their weapon over their head to show the pilots exactly where they wanted them to land, that was the normal procedure. "I had been to a party with most of these guys just a week or so before" Brink recalls. "For some reason, the RTO (Radio Telephone Operator) was this big Indian guy, (Native American) and was almost always the ground guide. Why they chose the biggest guy in the outfit to stand up in an LZ, I'll never know! It seemed like either myself or (WO1) Bob McKeegan were always flying first up when they got in trouble." Immediately as they touched down, Brink saw the ground guide "freeze" and then drop to the ground.

Brink called to the guys in the back to get the ground guide, and then, almost immediately, the crew of Dustoff 707 started taking fire. "We had to have landed in the middle of the bad guys, there were NVA

(North Vietnamese Army) all over the place but the good guys were there and it was a hell of a firefight" said Halvorson. Brink remembers the Crew Chief Johnson dragging the ground guide back to the aircraft and the Medic Crockett now found himself very busy on his side trying to get everyone onto the aircraft.

Halvorson looked out his windshield and saw an NVA soldier with an AK-47 pointed at him. "The guy could not have been more than 14 and he fired his whole magazine at us. Had I not been on the controls with Brink, I could have fired my .38 pistol at him and hit him without aiming, he was so close." The young enemy soldier was not done, however, and as Halvorson was congratulating himself on not being hit, the teenager loaded another magazine and emptied that one into the helicopter, too! Again, Halvorson got lucky and was not wounded, but as this was going on, things were heating up in the back of the Huey.

The LRRPS were jumping into the back of the aircraft while being shot at and the moment that Johnson got the ground guide on board, one of the LRRPs was hit in the head, sending blood and brain matter all over the inside of the aircraft, even onto the windshield.

"Apparently the round came from the back of the aircraft, through the engine compartment" Brink stated. At that exact moment when the soldier was hit by enemy fire, Halvorson caught movement out of the left corner of his eye; "Lt. Brink's legs were flying out and I saw his head slump forward. With all the debris on the inside of the windshield, I thought for sure Gary was dead. There was even hydraulic fluid spraying around the inside of the aircraft. It was one of those moments where I thought to myself 'Oh, shit, Oh, shit, Oh, shit!"

Lt. Brink picks it up from here, "A bullet came from behind and nicked my helmet, then exited out the front window. I went into a prenatal position, trying to take off looking through my chin bubble. At about the same time bullets hit my seat exploding ceramic shards into my legs, but I didn't realize it at the time. Bullets went between my legs, right past my cyclic, and into the radios.

What was strange was I can still see the bullets moving in slow motion into the center console. Realizing the situation we were in, I tried my best to assume the best possible fetal position I could, considering I needed to get my feet back on the controls! If I could have crawled inside my helmet, I would have!"

Gary Brink's helmet was grazed by a bullet from behind, "just as I tried to pull myself into that fetal position" he recalled. Had he not made that movement when he did, who knows what damage that bullet would have done to him.

In the back of the aircraft on the right side, Medic Frank Crockett has by now pulled his .38 revolver from his holster and has begun shooting in an attempt to protect the LRRPs who are also shooting and trying to scramble aboard the rescue helicopter on the right side.

On the left side, Crew Chief Tommy Johnson of Oklahoma began grabbing more bodies, pulling the one LRRP who is now dead, and then others, some of whom are now wounded, across the hard metal floor of the cargo compartment.

"Sometimes we had to stack them like cordwood" he remembered, but this time it was just get them on so they could get the heck out of there!

19-year-old Crew Chief Tommy Johnson

Back up front in the cockpit, with all the bullets flying around, Halvorson is thinking that he may be the only one of the crew left alive in the aircraft when he gets a slap on the back of his helmet from one of the LRRPs, shouting "GO,GO,GO!"

Of course, this entire rescue so far has taken place in maybe 10 to 15 seconds at the very most, but the Huey is still on the ground. It's time to pull pitch... Time to get out of Dodge City! Halvorson calls out, "Brink's been hit! I've got the controls!" At the time, Rob didn't realize it, but no one could hear him.

Whether it was because both pilots were actually on the controls or because there was still some hydraulic fluid left in the helicopter's system or whether it was pure adrenaline pumping through their bodies, Brink and Halvorson were able to lift the Huey out of the LZ, making a left turn as most of the NVA seemed to be to the right. A Huey with no hydraulic assist is like driving your car when the power steering goes out, only much harder. One pilot can work the controls when this happens but it is extremely difficult; two pilots on the controls are better, but it's still very difficult. Even though they were lifting out of the LZ, Crew Chief Johnson knew they were still in trouble. "The aircraft was all over the place as we took off." He could tell the pilots were having trouble with the controls; it was not a normally smooth departure.

And Johnson had his hands full, too; one of the LRRPs was not inside the aircraft yet when they took off.

With the soldier's feet on the skids and only one hand holding onto a litter pole, the other clutching his weapon, Tommy reached outside the aircraft and grabbed the guy by the belt to haul him in. "I was halfway outside the aircraft myself," he said, "but I was tethered in to the aircraft so I knew that *I* wasn't going anyplace! If that guy had lost his grip on the pole, he would have been a 'goner.'"

Clawing for altitude, Aircraft Commander (AC) Brink has difficult and sluggish controls and realizes he is also "kind of" fighting the Co-Pilot for the "advantage." Brink glanced to his right and says to Halvorson "Get your god-damned hands off the controls." Halvorson looked back at the AC "like he had seen a ghost" Brink said. Halvorson now realizes that Gary is, in fact, OK and is flying the aircraft, so he let's go of the controls. Without looking this time, Brink comes over the intercom again; "You're fighting me on the controls!" Halvorson speaks back over the intercom "I'm not on the controls" but now realizes that he is not transmitting, he can't hear himself in the headset; he can only hear the others.

Bullets in the radio compartment can do that! Again, Brink tells Halvorson he is fighting him.

So Rob holds up his hands towards the left seat, showing he is not on the controls. Brink looks over, and his reply? "Oh!"

Now out of immediate danger, but flying a very badly crippled Huey, Brink tries to call Quang Tri tower but gets no response. His radio is out, so he tells Halvorson "Call Quang Tri and tell them we need a straight in approach.

Tell them to clear the area and get the crash trucks ready. Have them call the hospital and let them know we're coming. We won't be able to land at the hospital pad" as he continued to fight the controls. Rob pulled the microphone away from his face and mouthed the words to Gary "I have no commo." Noticing that the AC is not quite understanding him, Halvorson pulls out his grease pencil, and finding a clear spot on the inside of the blood spattered windshield writes "I have no commo." As it turned out, not only did Rob have no commo, most of the instruments on the control panel were not working either.

In the cargo compartment of the Huey, Crockett and Johnson are tending to the wounded and they are trying to "take stock" of what they have on board.

Johnson, monitoring what is going on over the intercom, noticed the message on the windshield. "Why don't you use your survival radio, Mr. Halvorson?" Early in the history of the 237th, for over a year, DMZ Dustoff crews were short on equipment and had to fly these single ship, single engine aircraft rescue missions with no emergency radios whatsoever. But fortune was trying to smile on this crew, and Halvorson pulled out his emergency radio to call Quang Tri tower.

They needed a nice long paved runway to put this puppy down and their home base at "QT" was the ticket.

Grabbing the hand-held radio and transmitting on Guard, Halvorson alerted the tower to their situation. "This is Dustoff 7-oh-7 on Guard, north of Quang Tri about 20 miles out. We have multiple wounded on board, no idea of their condition, no hydraulics, and no instruments. We need a straight in. Clear everything, I need to be first in line." It was about this time that Gary noticed one of the few instruments still working was the engine temperature gauge "And it was running pretty hot!"

All appropriate measures were immediately taken by the tower controller.

Dustoff 707 was in serious trouble; they were fighting to stay in the air, yet they were still about 10 minutes away and limping home. Of course, transmitting on Guard alerted every other aircraft in the area and it wasn't long before the crew of 707 heard on their radio "This is Pachyderm 38, Dustoff, we're at your 9 o'clock and we're bringin' ya home!" Of course, it was somewhat comforting to know someone else was there.

Pachyderm was the call sign of the CH-47 Chinook helicopters that the 101st Airborne Division flew, and there was more to come. Soon the Huey crew also heard "Dustoff 7-oh-7, this is a heavy fire team at your 3 o'clock; were takin' you home, too, buddy!" Now they had 3 Cobras, a heavy fire team, covering their butts!

Halvorson remembers "There must have been 27 helicopters and fixed wings following us to QT. Yeah, I'm probably exaggerating the number a little, but not by much!" As they approached the runway at QT, the tower called back with landing approval and "The hospital wants to know how many wounded you have." "I don't know, several" was Halvorson's reply. "Just clear the runway."

Still very busy on the controls, Brink is setting up the Huey for a long, low approach to the runway, the best way to make a landing with no hydraulic power. The pilots continue their narrative.

"About the time we have the runway in sight, we get a call from this Command and

Control General from the 5th Mech," (5th Mechanized Division, which DMZ Dustoff supported for most of it's time in Vietnam). "He's in his Huey and is also following us. He's telling us 'Dustoff, this is Red Devil 6... Boys, just remember your training, just like in flight school. It's gonna be OK, Gentlemen, just rely on your training, you're going to do fine' and Rob is thinking 'Just be quiet and let us land the darn thing!'"

Well, the boys did remember their training and with both pilots on the controls, they were able to put the Huey down on the runway, skidding to a halt, skid shoes smoking and smelling of that distinctive odor all Huey crews remember from practicing emergency procedures such as this. They were able to put it down, under control, with no further damage. The 18th Surgical Hospital had their ambulances waiting and took care of the wounded.

Medic Frank "Davey" Crockett left the aircraft and accompanied his patients to the Emergency Room. While Crockett was put in for the Bronze Star for his actions on this rescue, I have lost contact with his family and do not know if it was actually awarded. Whether it was awarded or not, he certainly deserved it for his heroism in defending his patients.

Perhaps because of his actions during this mission, WO1 Robin Halvorson was made an Aircraft Commander the next day, having proved himself under heavy enemy fire.

Incidentally, other than the award for Crockett mentioned previously, there were no known medals awarded any of the other crew on this mission, mostly because they went into North Vietnam "illegally." But after all, even if they hadn't crossed "the river" they were only doing what they were supposed to be doing; it's what they were trained for. They were all volunteers and medals were not expected.

Medic Frank Crockett

1LT. Brink offered these additional comments on this mission, "The interesting thought that is not mentioned much is that poor wounded soldier who we had first picked up. I bet he avoided ever riding on a Dustoff helicopter again!"

And this, "I have always felt that Tommy and Davey were the heroes on that mission, going back and dragging the ground guide LRRP into the aircraft after he froze there at the nose of the aircraft.

As far as the bullet holes, many of the hits were in the underneath of the aircraft as the NVA were shooting as we were taking off." That same day, Brink filled out an after-action report, detailing the mission for headquarters. "It was tough.

I knew those guys we picked up and now at least one of them was dead. Some of them I had just met at the party." What was even tougher was this: when 67th Medical Group found out 7-0-7 had crossed "that river" they grounded him! He was temporarily not allowed to fly because he violated the agreement with North Vietnam. (Like the NVA honored the agreement!) But when Red Devil 6, a one star general, heard about the grounding, he overrode it and Brink was back in the air 2 days later.

Here is one of those times where memories differ. Halvorson stated, "I don't think we crossed the river this day. I'm not saying I never did, I just don't think we did this time."

Without a doubt, however, both agree that they were at *least* deep into the DMZ, whether they crossed the river of demarcation or not. Brink says they crossed, Halvorson says they didn't.

And speaking of 1LT Brink, remember those shards of his armored seat that knocked his feet off the pedals? Months later, Brink noticed his legs were itching a lot. While scratching them one time, he noticed that he pulled out a piece of the ceramic that surrounded his armored seat. "I didn't even realize those pieces penetrated the skin.

I was pulling stuff out of the back of my legs for years after that!" The seat was stopping the bullets but the rounds were disintegrating the coating and sending shards into his legs; he didn't even realize it at the time.

And the Helicopter? Oh, that! As a Huey is shut down, the normal procedure is to wait two minutes at a reduced RPM to let the engine cool down. Being the good pilots they were, Brink and Halvorson were waiting out the cool down period and at the two-minute mark, Rob cut off the fuel, shutting down the engine.

It was at this time, with no fuel forcing the engine to run, when the engine suddenly seized; "it just locked up," both pilots recalled. Looking at each other in disbelief, they couldn't quite figure out what had happened. As the crew performed a post flight inspection, they found the problem with the engine... There was no oil in it; a bullet had drained it all. Remember it was running hot on the way home? The engine had seized after shutdown, as good fortune had continued to smile on them; it just as easily could have quit in the air rather than on the ground. Further inspection of the aircraft also showed no transmission oil (the oil cooler had taken a hit) and no hydraulic fluid, as would be expected with the control problems.

Oh, yes, they counted about 100 bullet holes. While Halvorson remembers 121 hits, Brink says, "That seems a little high, but it was at *least* high double digits!"

Regardless of who is correct, they counted a whole bunch of incoming rounds in 6-2-7.

Since the Huey was still virtually intact, the common practice was to sling load it to the repair facility at Red Beach, on the west side of Da Nang Harbor, about an hour flight away.

Poor ol' 627 was rigged for it's inglorious ride South, having already served the 237th Medical Detachment for just under two years, and having flown for DMZ Dustoff a very honorable 1,212 hours. But at this post-flight part of the mission, we have another conflict of memories.

A few days after this last landing, and having saved literally thousands of lives over her career, 627 left the ground one more time as the Chinook that was sling loading her headed for the coast and the flight to Da Nang. Halvorson remembers that, "at about 100 to 150 feet, the aircraft broke free of the rigging and crashed back onto the airfield." But Brink remembers it differently. He says, "I was told that somewhere over the choppy South China Sea, 627 came loose and was lost over water, never to be recovered."

Regardless of who, or both, is correct, the fact is that she had at least one more hard landing. Although there is some "paper" evidence that 627 did fly again months later, it is highly doubtful, considering the amount of damage it received, even if it *wasn't* dropped. Regarding the sling loading of 237th Hueys, Halvorson had this to say, "As I recall the mast broke when it was slung, which was the reason it dropped.

I also remember the skids being massively sprung. Of course, I have slept since then, so who knows. As to whether it could have been slung more than once, I am sure it was. Having our birds slung out was a semi-regular occurrence for a while there."

Whether the loss of this very heavily damaged Huey occurred over land or over water or both is still uncertain at this time, 40 years later. Was it "punched off" over the water because it was dropped over the airfield or because it was so badly shot up that no one in Red Beach maintenance wanted this wreck taking up space? We just don't know for certain. Both pilots *could* be correct, but one thing is unquestioned; UH-1H 67-17627 *always* brought her crew home, even when she was terribly wounded.

Being dropped at either place or both, it was a fate she certainly did not deserve.

627 Being Hoisted From Quang Tri

One final note. When I started research-ing another mission, I was told about Crockett having to fire his weapon to protect his patients on this mission. I had to know more about what happened. But the pilot who told me about it wasn't sure who else was on board except Halvorson, and no one knew how or where to locate him. When I finally found Halvorson months later, he told me Brink was the AC and who the Crew Chief was. "I know the Crew Chief was TJ (Tommy Johnson) on this mission. He had that Texas drawl (Tommy says it's an Okie drawl, "it only *sounds* like Texas") and he carried this great big honkin' screwdriver in his tool kit, biggest one I ever saw. He used it to intimidate POW's when we picked them up. It was Tommy, for sure!"

When asked about the screwdriver, Johnson said, "We knew the POW's might go for our personal weapons and I didn't want any bullets flying around inside my helicopter, so I would just grab that screwdriver and make sure they saw it."   And that's no April Fool!

Mission 2
Saga of Captain America
DMZ Dustoff 713

One of the neat things about the assumption of Historian duties of the 237th Medical Detachment, DMZ Dustoff, has been locating former members of the unit, their photos... And their family members.

At the first reunion, Richard Villa (CO-host) and I received a "Thank You" from every family member in attendance that was related to someone Killed In Action, KIA. Because the results were so positive, Richard and I resolved to find the families of the KIAs we had yet to locate. In the early Spring of 2007, I was able to locate Dr. Jason MacLurg, brother of Medic David MacLurg, who was KIA on 27 September 1970. Dr. MacLurg sent me a collection of many photos that David had taken, and included were a series of 3 photos of a damaged 237th Huey. Inspecting the damage to the Huey in the photos was pilot WO1 Bob McKeegan, one of the most accomplished and respected pilots ever to come out of the 237th. The aircraft showed damage to the left windshield and left door plus the entire nose and windshield were covered with mud.

Most surprising to me, however, was a red, white and blue helmet that Bob was wearing in the photos!

Unfortunately, Bob died in a motorcycle accident in September of 2003, and I was afraid that the story of this aircraft might be lost, but his best friend in country, Dave "GoGo" Gomez, DMZ Dustoff 701, had the details. An email from me with the photos brought a swift and interesting reply from GoGo on 29 September 2007.

It follows,

"Phil,

Well... I have to go back to one night sitting at our outdoor theatre in Quang Tri watching a newly released movie, called 'Easy Rider.' Bob McKeegan was completely taken by the cool Captain America helmet worn by Peter Fonda in the movie, and was determined to also wear a similarly painted one. He spent a few days gathering up the required red, white, and blue paint, and meticulously pain-ting the bright stars and stripes on his helmet. When he was done, it looked great, but some-how looked out of place in a jungle warfare environment.

McKeegan inspecting the damage to his side of the aircraft.

On his next scheduled day to fly, Bob proudly wore the helmet on his early morning mission to fly a hospital transfer from Quang Tri to Da Nang. On the return flight from Da Nang, Bob flew the established low-level route at the departure end of Da Nang's runway, and under the departing traffic. Unfortunately, at the same time, an Air Force F-4 was departing and for some reason decided to maintain a very low level altitude after takeoff. Bob said that he looked over his shoulder just in time to see the low-level fighter coming right at him and made an abrupt evasive maneuver to barely avoid a mid-air collision. Bob was always Mr. Cool, but he was still pretty shaken up about it when he got back to Quang Tri an hour later.

Later that afternoon, Bob and his crew got a mission to pick up a downed flight crew. Sounded fairly routine until hearing that 6 other helicopters, from other units, had already tried to do the rescue pick up, but were turned away by heavy enemy fire and after receiving multiple aircraft hits. Bob and his crew flew in and successfully picked up the downed crew while also receiving heavy enemy small arms fire and accurate mortar rounds. Bob was able to fly to an area of safety before setting down to inspect the damage caused by several small arms hits.

Note bullet hole in left windshield under the wiper blade and damage to very top of door. Also, the mud on the nose and Red Cross is visible.

A/C 68-15691 due to black trim on Plexiglas.

I don't recall how many hits his aircraft took, but every bullet and mortar shrapnel penetration was on the left cockpit area.

It appeared as if the bad guys were aiming at his brightly painted helmet. Bob sustained a lot of small Plexiglas fragments imbedded in his face and was later awarded a Purple Heart for his wounds.

To this day, I still laugh when I think of the image of Bob jumping out of the helicopter, throwing his newly painted helmet to the ground, and swearing that he would never wear that f###ing helmet again. The very next day, Bob re-painted his helmet back to O.D. green."

Dave, Dustoff 701

The mortar rounds explained the mud on the front and now we know how the aircraft was damaged. Apparently, Medic David Mac-Lurg was on both those missions with Bob as the helmet painting only lasted for one day, the day David took these photos. One day in the war can be pinpointed by a little detective work and a little luck. One day in the Saga of flying Dustoff near the DMZ in Vietnam can be documented.

And the demise of one Captain America helmet can be forever recorded for history, regardless of how short-lived it was.

Mission 3

Nobody Taught Us That Stuff, But He Figured It Out Anyway, A story About Dave "Go-Go" Gomez, DMZ Dustoff 701 and Bob McKeegan, DMZ Dustoff 713

Two Southern California boys with a sense of adventure, they found themselves flying helicopters in the Vietnam War in 1969 and 1970. Sadly, Bob is no longer with us, so I could not interview him for this story, but Go-Go has recently retired from flying many, many years with the Los Angeles Police Department and offers us an insight into the bravery and audacity of Bob McKeegan.

Dave was "First Up" this day; Bob was "Second Up." First Up took the emergency missions while Second Up normally flew patient transfers or other similar "non-combat" missions, but was fully operational and fully crewed for virtually any situation except a hoist mission. With only one or two hoists in the unit, the hoist had to be installed on the first up aircraft each day.

As First Up Aircraft Commander, Gomez received the mission sheet and realized that there were too many casualties for one aircraft or lift. The unit was under fire and the wounded needed immediate evacuation, so McKeegan and his crew were pressed into action as well. Both aircraft cranked and departed at the same time, and while they were in route, Bob calls Dave on the radio. "Who's going in first?" was Bob's transmission. Dave answered, "I'm First Up so I guess I'll go first."

Arriving at the Landing Zone, Gomez made his approach and landing to the ground guide who was indicating where to land and where the wounded were. Getting in was uneventful, but shortly after touching down, mortar rounds began to impact around the aircraft. It was obvious that the bad guys were trying to walk the rounds onto the spot where the Huey was sitting and McKeegan, who was orbiting over the LZ, watching all of this take place, called out to his best friend "They're getting closer, you need to get out of there." Gomez replied, "We're almost ready" and only a few seconds later, he pulled pitch to leave the LZ with a full load of wounded.

But now the enemy had the Landing Zone zeroed in and Bob had to land in the same place to rescue the rest of the wounded... Bob and his crew were in deep trouble because that spot was now sighted. And here is the part they never taught us: Bob called the troops on the ground and told them to move their wounded to the other end of the LZ; "Call me when you are ready." He continued to orbit while Gomez also stayed in the area to make sure McKeegan got out in one piece. A few minutes later, he got the "All ready" from the guys on the ground. Bob shot his approach to the original spot, then waited a few seconds for the mortars to be launched at him. Waiting for what he felt was an appropriate few seconds, he then picked up the aircraft to a high hover and swiftly moved to where the wounded were newly located as mortar rounds began hitting where he originally landed. By the time the mortar tubes could be adjusted to their new target, the crew of DMZ Dustoff 713 had their patients loaded and were on their way out of the proverbial "harm's way." The bad guys had taken the bait; Bob had gambled and won.

Bob McKeegan was thinking on the fly, literally; not bad for a couple of 20-year-old surfer dudes from SoCal.

Bob McKeegan, left, Bob Carter, center, and Dave Gomez, right.

Photo taken the day Carter took McKeegan and Gomez to Da Nang for their DEROS flight back to America.

Mission 4

A <u>SMALL</u> SAMPLE
WHAT IT TOOK TO BE
A DUSTOFF MEDIC
Case in point:
Specialist Al "Jinx" Jenkins

Eight or nine weeks of basic training and then a 10 week Combat Medics Course at Ft. Sam Houston, Texas; you're away from home for probably the first time in your life, and it was something you volunteered to do. "What were you thinking?" But, then, that's how many Dustoff Medics started out in life, but once the training was all over, you were "68 Whiskey" Military Occupation Specialist (MOS) identification for a U.S. Army Combat Medic!

Al Jenkins was a typical FNG, "Funny" New Guy; 20 years old when he arrived in Vietnam, where most were 19 to 21 years of age and some were right out of High School. Twenty years old in Southeast Asia, but not old enough to vote or drink back in the "Real World" as we called it, back in the USA, but old enough to answer his country's call to duty.

He was eventually assigned to the 237th Medical Detachment (Helicopter Ambulance) in Northern I Corps, Vietnam, where I had the pleasure of flying with him. Like most, Al quickly made new friends in the 237th and soon learned the routine of flying into hostile landing zones several times a week, sometimes several times a day, all for the purpose of rescuing sick and wounded soldiers... As well as the dead. Dustoff crews were known to have a higher casualty rate than other helicopter missions as these UH-1H Hueys with the Red Cross were unarmed and usually flew completely alone... And "naked."

Al has many stories and memorable missions, I'm sure, but this is not an attempt to relate them at this time. This is only a brief summary to point out the mentality and dedication these Medics had, which, I believe, was typical of many Dustoff crewmembers, both Medics and Crew Chiefs. They knew that men in the field were depending on these rotary winged angels of mercy that they were part of, and they were willing to risk their lives to accomplish those missions. Their pay was minimal, only a few hundred dollars a month plus combat pay of 50 dollars and flight pay of 75. But, they did get free room and board!

Army soldiers were typically assigned to Vietnam for 1 year, 365 days; one could count them down one day at a time, and usually did. (The Marines had to do one better; they were assigned for 13 months!) Of course to shorten the time left in country, instead of, say, 200 days left, it was 199 days and "a wake-up." But Al was different, and he took advantage of an offer that if one voluntarily extended their tour to 18 months, they could leave the Army immediately upon returning to the US. This is what he did, serving his fellow soldiers for 6 more months, 6 more months than most "sane" people would have done!

What prompted this narrative was a brief mention to me in an email by Al about his last day in Vietnam. I pressed him for more details and while reading his reply, I found myself intensely proud of this gentleman that I now consider a good friend, not just someone I happened to fly with many years ago. Al simply told me that his orders to return home were past due, yet he was still flying missions:

On a true note... I came in after a mission and Conners or "the Nose" Fanelli came over to the bird with my DEROS (Note: Date of Expected Return from Over Seas) *paper work and I had been out of the Army for 3 days already.*

I said, "I quit" and just then we got a call to go out to somewhere and I cowboyed up one last time. I told whoever was at the stick to get another Medic 'cause we had a bird headed for Da Nang that afternoon and I was going to be on it. As much as I loved it I was wore out. 19 months in country and a year with Evans/DMZ and I wanted home. Got home and wanted to go back to the war... Isn't it funny how that all works out?

I again asked Al for further details of his last day, here's what he sent me in the next e-mail,

"I didn't have much time to get my shit in a bag let alone steal anything (like an M16) and I left my stuff to be shipped and left in a flight suit with papers in hand. I knew near the end I was used up, maybe not as sharp as I was when time was not the factor but I was never scared on a mission. I peed while refueling a bunch, though. I never thought those papers would come but I did know they were over due cause I was counting past short time. I think we had a real shortage of Medics or maybe I could have prepared for DEROS a little better, some compensation time may have been nice. Anyway I got to Da Nang, (67th Medical) Group dropped me off at the airport and I got on a C-123 to wherever.

I got on the silver bird with a bunch of two tour/E-5 and above folks that were all half nuts. Got off in Alaska for a couple hours dead tired and was in Washington (State) and out of the Army so fast my head was spinning. We may have refueled at Guam or Wake Island but it was all a sleepwalk.

No one would have thought any less of him had he stopped flying on "wake-up" day, yet he continued to fly day after day, knowing he was now on "his" time, not the Army's time. More so, he even took a mission with DEROS papers in hand! After 18 or 19 months, I know of very few people that would have done that; I have to stop and think whether *I* would have flown that last mission or not! But Al Jenkins did, and not only do I have MUCH respect for him as a Dustoff Combat Medic, because of his actions in serving his country, I have even more respect for him as a man."

Before closing this story, I have to add one bit of information that Al sent me AFTER I showed him the draft of this story. It's about his "DEROS Ride", the last flight a helicopter crewman gets in country, on his way back to the World. His narrative goes like this,

"The bird that was going for Hot End inspection, for some reason was AC'ed by Lt. Cox and I had a fly-by, some smoke wired up on the skids and he did either a fantastic or lucky fly by for me but I thought sure we were going right though the front door of the 18th Surgical Hospital. He was low rolling like thunder and pulled that bird up so hard I thought we had over-torqued it. Scared the piss out of me. For some reason Cox took that bird to Da Nang (Note: Apparently, Lt. Cox did not have his AC orders yet, but not unusual for an experienced Co-Pilot to be Pilot in Command) *and maybe I was over stressed but I recall the thought of crashing right into the Surg's front door as we zoomed just inches from the roof of the ER that morning. Lt. Cox had the bird that day and I about shit my flight suit. A fly by I'll never forget and pucker-up buttercup ride for sure. The rest of the ride was fine, maybe ole Cox was a better stick than I thought and he sure showed his stuff that day!"*

If only there were more people in the world like my good friend Al Jenkins. We all have much to learn from his attitude and his deeds.

Al in position with the hoist behind him

Al Jenkins And Gary Williams In Their Plywood Hooch

Mission 5

Legend Of "Crash" Carter
Tun Tavern: 1 June 1970
Geoffrey Morris' Silver Star
And
The Rescues At Fire Support
Base "Tun Tavern"

Researching this story was quite an eye-opener for me because I had no idea DMZ Dustoff had incurred so many losses at the same place and virtually at the same time. Had I not been wounded and sent home early as I was, I most likely would have been involved in the missions documented in this story.

Fire Support Base, FSB, "Tun Tavern" was located about 33 kilometers (klicks) SW of Quang Tri. From Wikipedia on the Internet, "According to tradition, Tun Tavern was also where the United States Marine Corps held its first recruitment drive. On November 10, 1775, the First Continental Congress commissioned Samuel Nicholas, a Quaker innkeeper, to raise two battalions of marines in Philadelphia.

The tavern's manager, Robert Mullan, was the 'Chief Marine Recruiter.' Prospective volunteers flocked to the place, enticed by cold beer and the opportunity to join the new corps." Hence, this was the naming of the Landing Zone where these incredible events took place. Although it was the birthplace of the Marine Corps, it turned out to be a death place for DMZ Dustoff helicopters and some of the most intense rescues for many of the crews.

We begin this story about FSB Tun Tavern with one of the principal characters...

PART 1
BOB "CRASH" CARTER

"Look, ya gotta realize, I was only the Co-Pilot in those 3 crashes!"

"Okay" I promised Bob, "I'll make sure your story includes the fact you were never the pilot in command in those 3 instances" so there you have it, right at the beginning! Actually, he really wasn't that adamant about it, but it's so much more fun to pull his chain a little!

Warrant Officer 1 Robert B. Carter arrived in Vietnam early in January 1970 and served his 12-month tour until January of 1971 with the 237th Medical Detachment, "DMZ Dustoff." Bob wonders how he was chosen to fly in that unit as he was one of the very few Warrant Officers to fly with the 237th who did not attend the "Condensed Army Combat Medic School" for Dustoff pilots at Ft. Sam Houston, San Antonio, Texas. Pilots with advance orders to fly Dustoff normally attended this school immediately after graduation from Flight School at Ft. Rucker, Alabama or Ft. Hunter-Stewart, Georgia; Crash was trained at Ft. Hunter-Stewart. "All I can think of is that they needed a replacement pilot and my name was picked when I got to the 90th Replacement Battalion in Long Binh" he states. Normally a 10-week course for the Army's combat Medics, the Medic School offered a shortened 5-week course for the pilots that would be flying Medevac missions. And that is probably what happened, he was chosen purely by chance.

The original 237th arrived in Vietnam as a unit on Thanksgiving Day, 1968, and for the most part, all of the original personnel had departed (with the exception of a very few enlisted men who extended their tour) by Thanksgiving, 1969.

The unit found themselves down to 4 Aircraft Commanders (ACs) and only 7 Co-Pilots, CPs, (lovingly referred to as "Peter Pilots") where the normal complement for a Helicopter Ambulance Medical Detachment was 13 pilots total, including at least 6 ACs. The ACs at Carter's arrival were LT. Gary Brink and Warrant Officers Rick Beam, Dave Gomez and Bob McKeegan. CPs were Cpt. John Hill, 1LT. Mike Cox, Warrant Officers George Rose, Al Gaidis, Don Study, Walt "Itchy Pink" Adams and Rob Halvorson. Captain Hill was the new Commanding Officer of the 237th and had not yet received his AC orders.

According to Bob, "We had several new pilots in the 237th and so few ACs, that we were not getting very much flight time, so they sent us to the 571st Medical Detachment in Phu Bai, near Hue, to make courier flights with their ACs." Courier flights or as the Assault Helicopter Units called them "Ash and Trash missions" were non-combat flights for just about any reason, to include patient transfers. It was an opportunity for the FNGs, Funny New Guys; to get some much needed stick time to hone their skills before their promotion to AC. It was on one of those very early courier flights that Bob earned his nickname.

(Some veterans substitute the word "Funny" for another word beginning with the letter "F.")

"We had gone to Da Nang to pick up some new nurses and doctors and I am thinking the new Executive Officer of one of our two units. It was a beautiful Sunday morning and as our usual custom, we were flying north along the beach back to Phu Bai. I was on the controls when out of nowhere a loud bang and then all was quiet. Of course, we immediately entered autorotation and the 571st AC says 'I got it.' With the full load, we landed a little hard and bent the skids up pretty badly, but everyone, and everything else, was OK. Later, when we returned to base, Medic David MacLurg *(Ed: who later died in September, 1970, in an aircraft accident)* started calling me 'Crash.'" It sucks to be the Funny New Guy. So while MacLurg apparently never claimed to be clairvoyant, more was to come as Crash began to solidify his new moniker.

Soon after this incident, Bob was flying with AC George Rose Yakush on a mission to pick up wounded in an unimproved Landing Zone (LZ).

Unimproved in that it was not completely cleared, having several tree stumps protruding throughout the LZ that prevented the aircraft from landing on the ground. Upon short final approach, with George on the controls, the aircraft settled into a hover over the stumps in the landing zone, and then directly onto a stump, which pierced the bottom of the aircraft! Medic Geoffrey Morris was on this flight and remembers it this way: "I was the Medic on his (Carter's) 2nd crash on the tree stump. We could not land so we were pulling a 'short hoist' (10-15 feet) when the engine failed & we landed on a tree stump that pierced the bottom & speared the aircraft right up to the ceiling. I remember it vividly as I was lying on the floor running the hoist. The tree (8-10 inches in diameter) ripped my pants & cut the inside of my leg about 4 inches below my crotch. I remember everyone was a little nervous because the blades were striking the trees in the LZ." Even at full throttle, the engine could not produce enough power to stay at a hover and the aircraft was now a semi-permanent part of the Landing Zone. George later told this author, "I lost power after we came to a hover, but the Crew Chief got really angry with me and blamed me for destroying his helicopter. I told him we lost power but he didn't believe me."

Later, after the aircraft was recovered, a bullet hole was found in the compressor stage of the engine and George was vindicated; but Crash Carter had now been in the front seat of his second, & more heavily, damaged Huey. But... Wait for it... The "best" was yet to come.

Bob "Crash" Carter, Age 22. Note "Peace" Symbol With American Flag On Helmet And .38 Caliber Smith & Wesson On His Hip

Fast forward a couple months later to June 1, 1970 and Crash is now flying with 1LT Mike Cox, the unit Executive Officer in aircraft 67-17671, one of the original 237th Hueys.

"We were on a mission to pick up one wounded ARVN soldier, Army of the Republic of Vietnam... The good guys. It was way out west at the edge of the A Shau Valley at a Fire Support Base on a ridge called 'Tun Tavern'. It was very early in the morning, at sun up. As we maintained radio contact with the Australian advisor on the ground, we were informed that we now had 2 wounded to pick up. As we got closer to the LZ, 2 wounded became 3." It now was obvious to the crew that the LZ was very hot and probably getting hotter!

1LT Mike Cox, sitting on the floor of the cargo compartment. Note the clamps for holding the litters, both fixed clamps on the pole and the clamps on straps. The straps were used to keep the cargo area open until needed for stacked litters.

Crew Chief Bobby Campbell and Pilot Crash Carter. Campbell is wearing jungle fatigues and Carter is wearing 2 piece Nomex flight suit. New aircraft has yet to have Red Crosses painted on. Photo by Kim Peters.

In an emergency, the most vulnerable time for a helicopter is when it is on short final approach for landing or immediately upon taking off. If the crew has airspeed or altitude or both, they can generally land a helicopter with no damage or at least a minimum of damage, depending on the terrain under them. But on final approach or while taking off, the aircraft has neither airspeed nor altitude and leaves no emergency options for the pilots except <u>try</u> to control the inevitable crash.

Carter explains the attempt at Tun Tavern; "We were on short final, only about 10 feet off the ground, when there was a loud bang on the left side of the aircraft. We had been hit by an RPG (Rifle Propelled Grenade) or a recoilless rifle round under the aircraft and all we could do was crash land on the ID panel they had laid out for us." The Crew Chief, Bobby Campbell, was wounded pretty badly in his back and LT Cox received minor wounds in the leg. Medic Geoffrey Morris and Crash were both unscathed by the incident, but the aircraft, lying on the ground, was still under fire from the enemy.

Of course, the crew beat the proverbial "hasty retreat" from the aircraft, but as they scrambled down the ridgeline opposite the enemy fire, Morris, the Medic, realized that Campbell was still in the aircraft.

Years later, Bob wrote in an email, *"The RPGs hit the ground to our left, peppering the left of the aircraft and wounding Cox in the leg and Bobby Campbell in the back. The aircraft fell from 10 ft or so... We lost ground effect or power or I have replayed those few seconds over and over. What should I... Could I... Have done differently? The collective is in my armpit, dust everywhere and screams from outside the aircraft.*

I unbuckle but my way is blocked by the armored seat extension. Fear, panic, struggle, then Morris is at my door. He opens my door and slides the panel back. I unass the helicopter and meeting Cox, we tumble downhill a few yards. I turn to the aircraft and see Geoffrey pulling Bobby from the cargo floor. The screams continue but we are together twenty yards below and behind the helicopter, outside of their perimeter. Think, then a second explosion, Morris and I return to the AC for weapons and his med kit. Things begin to slow down; maybe even a thought begins to register. A huge valley below us; faces and foxholes above and to the west. We went uphill."

As a healthy survivor of the shoot down, Morris returned to the aircraft to retrieve Campbell. More enemy weapons fire and an explosion greeted him at the aircraft, but Morris grabbed Campbell and was able to carry the seriously wounded Crew Chief down the hill. "We called in the gun ships and Cobras worked over the area pretty good. We sat on the ground for about an hour when Rose and Halvorson were finally able to pick us up. The Cobras escorted us home, back to Quang Tri" Carter said.

Cobra escort!   Note the folded litters that are stowed in the back of the cargo compartment.

It was on this mission that Medic Geoffrey Morris earned his Silver Star, a very prestigious award for an Army Medic.   The account of Morris' actions this day will be found in the accompanying Part 2 of this story "How Geoffrey Morris Earned His Silver Star."

Weeks after our initial interview for this story, Bob Carter offered a postscript "My part after the crash and return to the 18th Surg was or is not the story of heroes. I'm standing in the ER, two of my crewmembers on tables, Geoffrey hard at work assisting doctors, I have no aircraft... Snowy Lawrence, Aussie advisor, says you are coming with me.

I spend the day at MACV in QT and then the night with too much scotch. It's a blur and I have no memory of the next 24 hrs. I am not sure how I got back in the rotation. Peters and Stone (Ed. 237th Crew Chiefs) baby sat me for a long while, probably until they ETS (Expiration, Term of Service) in October."

Snowy Lawrence, Aussie Advisor Extraordinaire

"I guess the 101st guys got tired of looking at our helicopter sitting on that ridge, so eventually, they sent someone in to blow it up. They would see it and think somebody was in trouble." So again, Crash Carter is Peter Pilot in the loss of his 3rd and final, helicopter, a total loss this time. And while the rest of his tour was *relatively* uneventful, he did offer a few more "tidbits" about his tour. Bob offers this bit of insight:

"As an army helicopter pilot in Quang Tri, 1970, we were at the end of the aviation food chain. I was the Aircraft Maintenance Officer and test pilot because I had changed the spark plug wires in a V8 Dodge and it ran. No Flt. Ops., no weather. No one to ask permission from but each other. You ran to the A/C, cranked it up and looked a mile to the south to a lighted tower. If you could see the three lights you went. If you couldn't see any lights, you prayed and went. You told the control tower your intensions and he told you if the airfield was open or closed and you went.

As a new guy in country I couldn't see any lights on the tower one rainy night in February. I said, "God, are we going to fly in this?" The AC leaned over and said, "Yes"... "We won some, survived others and lost way too many... But we tried and we tried."

His next adventure, or should we say MIS-adventure, was flying at night for a pickup very near the DMZ, Demilitarized Zone, separating North and South Vietnam. By this time, Bob has earned his title of Aircraft Commander. "We were on one of those pickups with no moon and dark as can be. We knew the wounded were close to the DMZ, but not sure exactly where; we were relying on our FM homing to zero in on them."

The FM homing utilized an antenna on the top of the aircraft, the so-called "towel rack" antenna because it resembles a towel rack mounted on a roof rather than a wall. This allows the pilots to watch the Instrument Landing System vertical needle swing left or right during FM transmissions from the guys on the ground. Normally the needle would be centered, but when the FM radio was placed in the "Home" position, the needle would move left or right, showing the pilots which direction the transmission was coming from. Only problem is, it does not show distance, only direction, so it was very possible to over fly the LZ and not know it unless the guys on the ground told you were overhead.

Apparently, this is what happened here as Bob continues. "We kept looking and looking and could not see anything.

They said they were firing some flares but there was nothing to be seen. Finally, I decided that we were probably too close to the DMZ, so I started a 180-degree turn back south. About halfway through the turn, we spotted their flare way behind us. At that exact moment there was a big explosion right below and behind us. I don't know what it was, but someone had to be looking out for us."

They realized then that they were over North Vietnam and the bad guys were shooting something big at them. Had they not turned when they did, they quite likely would have been hit as the turn apparently threw off the aim of the enemy, leaving the aircraft and the crew unhurt. The rest of the rescue was routine, if one can call landing during the darkest of nights in a mountainous area with only a strobe light to guide you as being "routine."

One final facet of Crash Carter's tour needs to be recounted here, it also involves landing in the jungle at night. "1LT Brink came up with the idea of procuring some flares that the slick units normally dropped from altitude during night time operations."

One high ship during these multi-ship missions would have a full load of flares and the guys in the back would toss them out one at a time to light the area below. This "flare ship" remained at altitude and was responsible for timing the drops to keep constant light going for the other aircraft operating in and out of an LZ. "So our next night mission" Crash recalls, "we dropped a flare from altitude which was great, but then we had to do a fast spiral down to get to the ground before the flare went out.

It turned out to be a rather hazardous maneuver because there was no guarantee we could get on the ground before it burned out. Plus, we now had to go through the 'dead man's zone' in the light, where they could see us, to get to the ground." (Ed: the "dead man's zone" was referred to as anything above low level, nap of the earth flying, and anything below 1500 feet AGL, Above Ground Level. Above 1500 feet was considered out of the range of small arms fire.) So while the flare idea looked great on paper, and the LT's idea had merit, in practical use it proved difficult and it seems that it was not used very often.

In all, Crash said he got most of his flight time in April, May and June of 1970.

"That's when we were the busiest," he says. "I probably got 40% of my total flight time those 3 months, the rest was comparatively quiet. In fact, I only got about 10 hours my last month of flying. But I remember sitting in Da Nang waiting for my flight home. I saw all these helicopters headed north and I remember saying to myself, 'I bet they are going to have some fun.'" Fun indeed, as these were the aircraft headed north from Chu Lai and other points south; they were headed for Khe Sanh and operation Lam Son 719.

Arguably the most ill conceived offensive operation mounted by the US and ARVN troops during the entire war, Lam Son 719 saw many, many good men die and many, many good helicopters destroyed, seemingly for naught. Entire volumes have been written about Lam Son 719, the 1971 offensive into Laos, and the reader will get another idea of what it was like to fly helicopters in Vietnam by reading about it.

Bob "Crash" Carter's tour could probably be summarized as being typical of most Dustoff crews in the 237th. "Hours and hours of boredom punctuated by moments of sheer terror" is how it's been stated by others before. It's not too far from the truth.

However, one thing this author has found in every Dustoff crewmember he has talked to; there is an intense sense of pride in having served in a Dustoff unit, and the feeling that, despite our losses, it was worth it. Pride in what we did and how we did it... Sometimes we still wonder just how DID we do it? And "get away with it?"

PART 2

HOW GEOFFREY MORRIS
EARNED HIS SILVER STAR

MEDICS JUST DOIN' THEIR JOB

There is a quote in the book "Dustoff" by John L. Cook that goes like this:

"Captain, you have to understand, if we gave Dustoff a medal for every heroic action, all we would be doing is giving Dustoff medals. It requires a certain amount of heroism just to fly in Dustoff, and they have to reach a higher bar." This quote comes from a MACV Lieut. Col., Vietnam, August, 1967, to Capt. Craig Honaman, Dustoff unit awards officer on why two Silver Star awards were downgraded to Distinguished Flying Crosses.

So with that little bit of background, we continue the mission on which Geoffrey Morris earned his recognition.

As was shown already on this day, the pilots up front were Warrant Officer 1 Bob Carter and 1st Lieut. Mike Cox with Crew Chief Bobby C. Campbell sitting on the cargo floor behind Lieut. Cox.

Medic Morris was sitting on the right side of the cargo floor behind Carter, their usual positions. No need to repeat the details of the crew being shot down, that has already been established in Part 1. For his actions on this mission, Geoffrey Morris was awarded the Silver Star for heroism, a very prestigious award for a Dustoff Medic or any Dustoff crewmember for that matter. His citation reads thus:

For gallantry in action while engaged in military operations involving conflict with an armed hostile force in the Republic of Vietnam. Private First Class Morris distinguished himself on 1 June 1970 while serving as Medical aid man aboard a helicopter ambulance during a rescue operation in a fire swept area near Hue.

As Private Morris and his companions attempted to land to evacuate several wounded allied soldiers from the scene of heavy fighting with enemy troops, their helicopter was severely damaged by hostile fire and forced to make an emergency landing in the contact area. Realizing that an explosion and fire were highly probable, the crew immediately departed the helicopter amid the hail of enemy fire. Moments later, Private Morris discovered that the Crew Chief was still on board the damaged ship and immediately returned to aid his companion.

Although intense enemy fire swept the area surrounding the wreckage, he ran to the helicopter and removed his injured comrade seconds before the aircraft burst into flames. After administering first aid to all injured crewmembers, Private Morris again exposed himself to the intense enemy fire as he searched the adjacent area for Allied ground combat troops. After treating several casualties, he ensured that all the injured were safely aboard a second evacuation helicopter that arrived on the scene a short while later. Private First Class Morris' gallantry in action was in keeping with the highest traditions of the military service and reflect great credit upon himself, his unit, and the United States Army.

Medic Geoffrey Morris At Work. Notice he is wearing an armored vest with no other protection and he has an extra equipment bag under the seat.

It must be noted here that it was several conversations over 4 or 5 <u>years</u> before Geoffrey Morris divulged that he had even received the Silver Star.

It then took more than one relentlessly applied request, coated with gentle persuasion, to get this citation from him, a man that this author has found to be quite humble and also a wealth of historical information during his time with DMZ Dustoff. Along with his Silver Star citation, Geoffrey also sent the transcript of a speech from Alan Rhodes, a commissioned officer who flew with the 237th. The speech is titled, *"Heroes I Have Known"* and was presented to a graduating class of Army Medics and their families. In his speech, he noted three Army Medics, two of which he flew with in Vietnam. Here is an excerpt from that speech,

"...My second hero was Specialist 4 David MacLurg. David was on duty one rainy, dark night when an urgent mission came in. A Vietnamese child, two years old, had turned over a pot of hot water severely scalding him, producing nearly 85% second-degree burns.

The prognosis for the child was not good with the prevalence of infection and lack of sophisticated burn therapy. The crew never once questioned whether they would or should try. After several attempts they reached the landing zone and picked up the child. On the return flight from the hospital they crashed.

About two hours later, I discovered the missing aircraft and landed, expecting the worst. David MacLurg was killed in the crash.

I carried his body to my helicopter and returned to home base.

During the next several days, as we grappled with the grief of losing one of our unit members, I realized David was a hero also. He didn't pause to ask if he should go, he didn't hesitate. He didn't say it doesn't matter, the child will die anyway. Specialist David MacLurg answered the call when someone needed help, without regard for his self. David's name is on the wall in Washington DC at the Vietnam Veterans Memorial."

"My third hero is specialist Geoffrey Morris. Geoffrey was a drill sergeant's nightmare. Long hair, parted down the middle, granny glasses. He looked the part of the stereotype troublemaker, but he taught me a valuable lesson about dedication to mission.

Our tours of duty in Vietnam were one year, 365 days long. We counted down the days until we left, from the new guy with 360+ long days to the short timer with only a few days left.

Specialist Morris was a short timer, with less than 10 days left when the South Vietnamese army invaded the country of Laos *with the objective of cutting the Ho Chi Minh trail, the major pipeline of supplies coming into South Vietnam. (Ed. This was Operation Lam Son 719.)*

My unit provided Medical evacuation coverage for that invasion, and Geoffrey Morris was a member of the unit. He could have stayed hiding in the base camp due to his short timer status, but no, he answered the call. He had already turned in his gear, his flight suits, his helmet, but that was no hindrance. He scrounged gear, found an aid bag, and climbed on the first available helicopter. It was chaotic during the first days of the invasion and I was the operations officer. That left me little time to account for the soldiers in my flight section. When I got around to taking a head count several days later, I was astonished when I saw Morris. He hadn't been able to scrounge any flight suits, so there he was in blue jeans; flying in the most intense anti-aircraft fire we had experienced, answering the call. Morris was past his rotation date, that day that each of us lived for, to catch the freedom bird back to the States.

I didn't understand why, so I asked him. His reply, 'Sir, you needed me.' Geoffrey answered the call with a dedication I had not seen before. With him, as well as with David MacLurg, it was service before self, answer the call. That is why these soldier Medics, graduates of this same course you are graduating from, are heroes I have known."

Geoffrey Morris, Medic, Silver Star Recipient

New, at the time, Pilot Bob Carter has one memory of Geoffrey Morris that he shared with this author.

"The Geoffrey story I like to tell is I'm the new Aircraft Commander and at the end of a mission I'm telling the FNG (Co-Pilot) all about my superior skill and experience while filling in the log book. I break my pencil and tell Geoffrey to go get me another. He says he is busy and that I might get my own pencil... I turn in my seat (with) my mouth open to speak and... Geoffrey and the Crew Chief are covered in blood, mucking the gore and pieces and parts off the deck. I learned a valuable lesson and hopefully passed it on to others... Thank you, Geoffrey..."

PART 3

1 AND 2 JUNE 1970, NO ONE WITH THE 237TH DIED THESE 2 DAYS BUT, BOY, WAS IT COSTLY!

FSB "Tun Tavern", the subject of Cox and Carter being shot down on June 1st (Part 1), was manned by South Vietnamese Infantry supported by an Australian Advisor.

We pick up the story of Tun Tavern from Hal "Stoney" Stone, a Crew Chief originally assigned to the 477th Aerial Rocket Artillery, the Cobra Gunships called "Griffins" which flew for the 101st Airborne Division.

Stoney, Kim "Sweet Lips" Peters and Bobby C. Campbell were all Cobra Crew Chiefs, but because the Cobra has just two tandem seats for the pilots, the Crew Chiefs can only fly very rarely, if ever. So the three Crew Chiefs, who had gone through virtually all of their Army careers together, extended their 365-day tours by 6 months so they could fly. They volunteered to fly Dustoff so they could get some "air" time. During an interview for this story, Peters offered this bit of insight:

"Do you know why they called me 'Sweet Lips?'" I was almost afraid to ask, but I let him continue, anyway. "When I would close the pilot's doors before a mission, I would blow them a kiss for good luck, so Halvorson started calling me 'Sweet Lips!'" Only in a combat zone!

Stoney is the Crew Chief for George Rose Yakush and Rob Halvorson as they pick up Cox, Carter, Campbell and Morris from Part 1. After returning the downed crew and the wounded to the 18th Surgical Hospital at Quang Tri, Stone and his crew were called back to Tun Tavern for more wounded.

Knowing the situation, they married up with the Griffins, the same Cobra pilots that the three Crew Chiefs had "wrenched" for just months before. The Huey came in low and fast, flying up a ravine that gave them some degree of protection, and popped up onto the ridge to make their pickup as 4 Cobras gave them cover. At the time, they didn't realize it, but they were being shot at with small arms fire as they made their low level approach. What they *did* realize is that as soon as they touched down, mortars began hitting all around them. Stoney remembers, "We headed to Tun Tavern. As we approached, I could see smoke.

The helicopter was on fire, on it's side. We landed and loaded Carter, Cox, Morris, Bobby C. and other patients. We returned to the 18th Surg. That was the last time I saw Bobby C." The wounded were loaded and the Dustoff departed, but the aircraft sustained some minor small arms damage and shrapnel from the mortars. Off to the hospital again when another call comes in... Tun Tavern has more wounded!

Huey cargo compartment: Crew Chief sat on the left, Medic on the right. Medic's flight vest is lying on the floor, ready to be put on at a moment's notice. Aid kit is a compartmentalized cardboard box! Crew Chief has discarded ammo box for his tools and some weapons he has scrounged from previous missions. Crew sits on 18-inch armor plates covered in Army blankets for comfort. Same plates are strapped to 18-inch doors for some small degree of side protection. Extra ammo and pilots' rifles can be seen hanging on armored seat backs. The blankets wrapping the armor plates could also be used for the patients if necessary. Photo By Geoffrey Morris

A helicopter in an LZ instantly becomes a high value target, and the enemy seized the opportunity to drop additional ordinance on Tun Tavern to try to take out another Medevac helicopter. The additional mortars launched into the Fire Support Base created more casualties and they had to go back!

As it turned out, they went back several times and every time they landed, they would take small arms fire on approach and mortars upon landing. And each time they returned, it created more wounded. On one of the pick-ups, Stoney remembers catching movement in his peripheral vision, "It was a body flying when a mortar hit next to him. All in all, we made 9 trips to the LZ that day, each time with the Griffins and each time we took fire and picked up more wounded." Incredibly, with some Plexiglas shot out and many hits on the aircraft, nothing critical was damaged and they continued to fly the same aircraft all day. "Each time, we went in with the Cobras' and each time we took hits," said Stone.

"I remember talking to the Cobras on the way back and forth to the LZ." These were the men Stoney had served with earlier and although it was rarely utilized, the crew in the cargo compartment had the ability to transmit and receive radio calls.

Hal Stone, Crew Chief

"Finally it got to the point that we just couldn't fly the aircraft anymore" Stone continues, "so Kim Peters and his crew flew in to make a pick-up at the LZ the next day. They got shot down on the first attempt!"

Crew Chief Kim Peters At Left Keeping A Watchful Eye And Dustoff 705, Rob Halvorson In Flight

2 JUNE 1970

PART 4
THE LOSS OF ANOTHER HUEY

Rob Halvorson remembers the details of being shot down. "I don't remember the date or the helicopter (Ed: tail number 69-15131).

A battalion of ARVNs were put in to reopen Tun Tavern and got the crap beat out of them.

I heard that the entire battalion staff was killed or wounded the first day and replaced.

I know that the slicks were hauling in replacements while George was hauling the wounded out the first day. There was a ravine running down the mountain to the river from the top. We would get in that ravine and roar up to the top. When you got to the top there were two pads and you could pick whichever one felt lucky."

"Walt Adams and I were first up the next morning. We had a bird that I think that he and I picked up in Saigon when it was brand new. Al Gaidis and I got the AC's rudder pedal shot off of it at LZ Charger down in Da Nang's AO. It had less than 50 hours on it when Walt ("Itchy Pink" Adams) and I broke it."

Walt "Itchy Pink" Adams

"As I recall the highest ranking ARVN was an NCO and there was one Australian advisor on the ground. The majority of the ARVNs were walking wounded. We came flying up the ravine and picked the pad on the right side. We landed at the same time as several mortars also landed and the ship went over and broke the main shaft. They drilled into you in flight school to always kill the battery if you were going in so as not to catch fire. As we started rolling over I killed the battery. Unfortunately the engine didn't die and without power you can't depress the solenoid that keeps you from rolling off the throttle to kill the engine. So the engine kept running.

Walt and the guys in back went out the right side, which was now the top. I was on the bottom so I decided to break the windshield and go out the front. That thing is a lot tougher than you would think. At one point I was beating on the Plexiglas with the butt of my pistol 'til I realized where the barrel was pointing every time the pistol made contact."

"I made my way into the back of the helicopter and there were 3 ARVNs there.

One was just sitting there and I picked him up, lifted him over the side and dumped him, the second one I had to catch because he didn't want to leave. The third guy was pinned by his legs and right shoulder by the helicopter when it went over. I couldn't be sure if he had a pulse or not. I was worried about him burning when the ship caught fire and actually had my pistol out while I was debating the morality of shooting him to keep him from suffering. At that point I realized that I was standing in a deep pool of JP4 (Ed. Jet Fuel) and that while he was unconscious, I was not. So I decided that he was on his own and I left."

"The first place I came to when I bailed was a conex (Ed: metal military shipping container) with a bunch of wounded in it.

I asked them as best I could who was in charge and they indicated that it was me. I declined and spotted a foxhole with an ARVN corporal with a radio in it. I ran and jumped into his fighting position and asked if I could use his radio. He graciously consented and I made a call telling the world that we were down and needed to be picked up. I heard an Australian voice say something to the effect of, "Dustoff 705, X-ray Zulu 36... We have everything under control and we will take care of you!"

Now at this point we were taking mortar fire, machine gun fire and there were Cobras working out overhead. I looked and saw the rest of the crew in a fighting position a little ways away and near them was another Caucasian working a radio. I jumped up, ran over and jumped into his fighting position. I stuck out my hand and said, 'Dustoff 705!' and he replied, 'X-ray Zulu 36' and I knew I was screwed."

Fire Support Base Tun Tavern In Northern South Vietnam, Photo by Kim Peters

"After things calmed down a little bit Walt & I recovered my helmet and sunglasses from the helicopter and we made contact with DMZ Dustoff. We tried again to kill the engine and debated turning on the battery long enough to roll off the throttle and decided not to. (Ed. So apparently, this Huey lay there on its side, engine running, until it ran out of fuel. That *could* have been an hour or more!) George agreed to pick us up but since my bird was occupying one of the pads we decided it would be better to be picked up further down the ridgeline outside the wire.

We had a bunch of walking wounded with us, Walt had one ARVN piggyback and I was carrying the Aussie's secure radio. We went out the wire and down the hill immediately outside the wire. When we got to the bottom the Aussie said, "Take care! That's where we took our last push from!" Really made me feel better.

There were dead NVA all over the place and we were in tall elephant grass. Walt spotted a Chicom pistol but figured it was probably booby-trapped and left it. He told me he tried to get one of the wounded ARVNs to grab it but they wouldn't.

We made our way out to the end of the ridge expecting to get fired upon at any time even though there were Cobra's and Loaches overhead. We got to the end, George swooped in and picked us up and gave us a hard time for having to do it. Something about him flying all day without getting hit and we can't even do it once. I am afraid I can't give you the details because I gave the microphone jack back to the Crew Chief when Rose got all cranked up."

Walt "Itchy Pink" Adams gives us his perspective of the incident, "The aircraft that was blown up was the only chopper lost that day, as far as I know.

As to a chopper making multiple pickups from one place, I do believe that would have been George Rose and one of the new pilots that got killed with Bob Hill (Warrant Officer Mike Bradley). George Rose had on one day (Ed. June 1st), evacuated many ARVN from Tun Tavern. Rose had the only co-pilot available at that time, Bradley.

The following day, Halvorson and I were flying the 1st up missions as AC and Pilot. We started out early the following morning. After loading many patients, while attempting to leave, we took incoming mortars. I believe the first hit was on the horizontal stabilizer, which did not stop us; the second one was on a rotor brace, SCREWED THINGS UP A BIT. I got wounded, and was awarded the Purple Heart by the 18th Surgical Hospital. There were no 4 cobras escorting us on *our* missions EVER, that I remember. I think I have seen a Cobra, and some Charlie model gunships, some Air Force Jets, but 4 Cobras, not to my recollection, not on this day.

When Halvorson and I got blown up on Tun Tavern, we endured the mortar barrage, and when we got fire support, it was from the Air Force Jets. Then we contacted DMZ Dustoff; and Yes, Rose was the man of the hour, and our crew departed Tun Tavern, down the ridgeline, over the dead NVA soldiers, over to another spot where Rose picked us up.

Halvorson carried a secure radio set, I carried a severely wounded ARVN soldier, and

710

Warrant Officer George Rose Yakush
DMZ Dustoff 710

the Crew Chief and Medic, made safe observations as we transitioned from Tun Tavern over to a place where Rose picked us up.

Warrant Officer Mike Bradley

Crew Chief Kim Peters had this recollection of being shot down,

"On June 1, 1970, Hal Stone's ship responded to evacuate the crew of Mike Cox, Bob Carter, Geoffrey Morris and Bob Campbell, who had been shot down near Tun Tavern.

Bob Campbell had been wounded severely and was brought back to the hospital. Bob was later evacuated to Japan for Medical attention. Hal and crew then took over for the first up position that day and my ship moved into support – second up. Hal made about 9 Evac trips that day out of Tun Tavern. At the end of the day, Hals' bird was full of holes and lost Plexiglas, but nothing critical had been hit. He related to me that evening, since I would be first up the following day, that the LZ in the firebase was a VERY hot spot, was zeroed in with rockets and mortars by the NVA and that when I went in, not to set my skids on the ground and not hover in one spot. Just get in and out and let the wounded get on (which they would).

The next morning it was our turn to start making the evacuations from Tun Tavern. Our first mission for the day took us on a standard tactical approach. At sufficient elevation, my pilots (Halverson and Adams) evaluated the LZ and options for approach. Then, we flew a few miles away and dropped down to treetop level height, following a valley. We flew as fast as possible at this elevation and followed the valleys and ravines they had noted previously to get into the LZ.

We came up a valley, then followed a large ravine that led directly to the firebase and LZ, popped up over the perimeter and positioned ourselves on a clear spot on the right side of the LZ, at which time I made a grievous error. I didn't do what Hal had told me to do, but allowed my pilots to do the standard thing and touch our skids on the ground, time frame, maybe 5 to 10 seconds. Evacuees loaded during that same time frame I estimate at around fifteen to twenty. I signaled my pilots to clear the LZ and my pilots brought our bird up to about a 3-foot hover preparing to take off. That's when they hit the LZ with mortar rounds. My ship immediately rolled over. So fast it never even registered.

When a helicopter rolls at that low of height, the rotors, which are each 25' long, hit the ground fast and then ALL hell breaks loose. The next thing I consciously remember was lying on the bare ground with the helicopter side door surrounding me (my bird was laying on its side). The turbine engine (located about 4' away from me behind a bulkhead) was still running at full throttle, but *without the added sound of spinning rotors, seemed quite eerie. I tried to get up but I couldn't move my legs. I immediately assumed that the helicopter was laying on them.*

I was also covered with pretty much all the gear in the helicopter which amounted to quite a bit: Medical supplies, body bags (these were uniquely quite heavy), armor plates, ammunition for all the unauthorized weapons we carried (for just in case) approximately 20 plus wounded and there was JP4 aircraft fuel leaking like crazy (to name just a bit of my problem). The initial thoughts that flashed through my mind were: pinned under the helicopter, engine still running, fuel leaking, under attack, going to catch fire shortly, going to burn to death, where is my 38 and do I have the guts to pull the trigger? Within seconds however, more positive thoughts came to mind like – Bull Shit... How do I get out of here? Later my Medic, Jim Manderville (who had climbed up the now vertical floor of the helicopter and out through his side door which was now the ceiling) said he stopped and looked back to check on me (and the mess covering me) and said I looked back up at him and just gave him a 'thumbs up" so he assumed I was OK and kept going. (I don't remember doing that.)

Very shortly some of the load laying on me was removed – specifically many of the wounded ARVNs' who were abandoning ship as fast as they could.

Once their weight was gone, I found that, with some sort of super power I didn't know I possessed, I was able to move my legs. With that little bit of information, I saw just a spark of hope for my future. In short order I was able to throw enough of the gear off me to be able to get up. Now I am standing on the ground surrounded by a helicopter with a turbine engine still screaming next door, standing in a growing puddle of JP4 and looking up the flat vertical cargo floor to the edge of the door-way. My exit strategy was to simply climb up this aluminum floor (which had no hand holds) and depart the scene as best I could. As I initially attempted to do this, others in the same predicament (a few remaining evacuees) also saw an opportunity. They saw the back of this relatively tall American kid (at least taller than them) who looked an awful lot like a ladder. Before I could even realize what was happening, I was assaulted from behind by several terrified individuals who used my back to scale an otherwise daunting obstacle.

Once most of them had made their exits, I found myself with just a few remaining others who seemed to be making other plans (and headway) on exiting the aircraft and I was able to concentrate on my own survival.

Again, with those unknown super powers I didn't know I had, I seem to remember "vaulting" over the top of that floor rim, landing in a ball on open ground and, knowing that the bad guys had this place zeroed, ran my scared little butt off to the nearest bunker. I was soon able to find the CP "trench" (Command Post), which was manned by some Australian advisors, and was able to hook up with the rest of my crew. We had all survived (so far) with no injuries. I found out later that one of my pilots, Rob Halverson, had still been in the ship when I got out. He was evidently trying to pound his way out through the front windshield with his 38 revolver. The call was made for a backup Dustoff and while we waited, we watched a very interesting Air Force Zoomie mission dropping napalm along the valley floor.

Eventually, our relief came in the form of my good friend Hal Stone and crew who had, since I guess they knew what it would take to support this location, had evidently "volun-teered"(?) to come to our rescue.

After a short radio conference, it was decided that our unit could no longer support evacuations from this LZ. One reason was because the enemy had it zeroed in too well and the other was because there was now a helicopter lying on its side in the LZ leaving no other room.

We agreed to cross through the wire outside the perimeter of the firebase to the north (I think) and follow the ridge a short way to what appeared to be a clear spot on the ridgeline. We did this, taking several of the wounded with us, and were able to make it to the new designated LZ. Following our original flight approach, our rescue bird came up the same ravine we had, but just prior to getting to the original LZ, they made a right turn near the ridge line and entered the new LZ. We were able to get ourselves and the wounded we had with us on to the bird while the original LZ was taking some heavy mortar hits. Just because the bad guys had the Firebase zeroed didn't mean they could see what was happening. This new LZ functioned as the only LZ for the next several days with no other ships hit. This was my third time shot down in Vietnam."

**Specialist Kim Peters, Crew Chief
Note .38-pistol and survival knife at the hip.
Bell on left breast pocket is good luck charm.**

Like so many vets, after 40+ years, Kim Peters remembers it like it was yesterday.

As a side note, Hal Stone recalls a time that they had to spend the night at a FSB deep in "Charlie territory" with 2 Cobras. The Base was quite regularly under fire and they wanted the gunships there and ready to go at any time.

Normally the gunships would show up at daybreak from their base, but this time was different, they were on the ground, waiting. On this night, the enemy attacked again, and as the Cobras started their engines, Stoney says he could hear the bad guys yelling, "deety mao" which loosely translated is Vietnamese for "Get the heck out of here, now!"

The enemy had a great fear of the Cobras, but never enough fear to keep them from shooting back when they could! At least this time, only the starting of the engines broke up their impromptu party.

So there you have it; Bob Carter solidifies his "Crash" nickname at Tun Tavern and we have now re-created the events of 1 and 2 June 1970 at the same LZ. We called it "Indian Country." The enemy lived there, controlled it then and always would control it. We were playing in his backyard and he wasn't very happy about it. But we were fighting a limited war; the North Vietnamese and Viet Cong knew that all they had to do was wait us out, they knew that we would eventually leave. They moved troops and supplies through Laos and Cambodia with impunity while we were not "allowed" to go there.

In 1973, the last US troops finally left South Vietnam and 2 years later, in 1975, the country fell to the Communists. It seems that all these losses were in vain; it is up to Historians to decide if that was the case.

**"Indian Country" Very Beautiful
But Also Very Hostile During The War**

Mission 6

George Rose Yakush
DMZ Dustoff 710

Some time ago, I sent an email to Warrant Officer Pilot George Rose Yakush about something I had read on the internet. A portion of that email goes like this:

I read somewhere on the internet about someone (a grunt?) who was talking to a Medic on a mission... I think it was the 237th... about "Thanks for getting us out" or something to that effect and the Medic told him, "This is our third aircraft this week..." Had to be Crash! I do know that he pierced the belly on one ship on a stump and I don't recall what happened to the second, but I think he went through two in one week. They may be related.

Here is his reply,

"711

I was actually the one that landed on the stump. I am not sure, but I think Crash was my pilot. I lost power on short, short final in a hover, LZ filled with stumps about 4 to 5 feet high.

When we hit the stump the Crew Chief wanted to know why I did it. We wound up getting hoisted out by a 571st aircraft because our 2nd and 3rd up ships were flying missions. I was the last one up on the hoist and I could see muzzle flashes coming from a bunker as I rode it up. They later hoisted my ship out and delivered it to maintenance where we found one small hole in the engine compartment. A round hit the compressor stage of the engine which explained why I lost power but the engine was still running. I'm not sure but I think the photo of the Chinook slinging one of our ships is of the ship I flew that day.

I seem to recall that Bob was involved in a lot of mishaps when he was a pilot but that he went through his career as an AC without a scratch – which would be very ironic for a guy nicknamed Crash.

We did have a period where all of our ships were either down from enemy fire or destroyed. Lycoming was on strike at the time and no new Hueys were coming to Vietnam. We borrowed ships from the 571st and got them shot up. We even borrowed a ship from Qhi Nhon and had that one shot up too. Gilliam sent me down to Bearcat, south of Saigon, to pick up a ship that the 1st Cav was going to transfer over to us.

It was a bullet ridden patched up leaking dog. I refused the aircraft and the 1st Cav unit Commander was pissed demanding I take the aircraft. It finally took setting up a land line call to Gilliam to get me out of Bearcat. I told him I wouldn't fly a mission with this aircraft and that was all he needed to hear.

When we finally got a few new ships in, we started flying them in the field before the break-in period was over. I was flying one with only 60 hours on it and no red crosses. I repeatedly asked the Crew Chief to paint some white boxes and red crosses on the ship since there wasn't much activity that day. Later in the day I finally gave the only direct order I gave to the Crew Chief to paint at least one white square with a red cross. He did. He painted it on the nose of the aircraft. Just around dusk, we received a mission to pick up a wounded green beanie (Ed. Green Beret) west of Khe Sanh. It was hot and as we came in on short final something hit me in the leg and knocked up off the pedal controls. It turns out that a round came up through the floor, hit something, and split. Half of it hit my left thigh and the other half went through the green house. Fortunately the part of the round that hit me was slowed down.

It penetrated the skin and just scratched the muscle and left a black and blue mark the size of a volley ball on my leg. We later figure the trajectory of the round and considering the forward movement of the aircraft, it appears that the bad guy was aiming at the red cross on the nose. And so were some of the perils of... 710."

George Rose Yakush, DMZ Dustoff 710

Mission 7

Charlie Whaley, Specialist
My Most Memorable Mission

Special Orders Number 893 dated 16 April 1970, Vietnam, read like this,

For heroism not involving actual conflict with an armed enemy in the Republic of Vietnam: Specialist Five Whaley distinguished himself while serving as Crew Chief aboard a helicopter ambulance during a rescue mission near Dong Ha just south of the Demilitarized Zone. He and fellow crewmen had been requested to pick up the pilot of a Marine helicopter gun ship shot down by enemy ground fire. When the rescue team arrived over the wreckage, they found that the gunship had crashed in a small ravine too narrow to accommodate the air ambulance. The pilot then hovered down the side of the ravine as close to the wreckage as possible, and Specialist Whaley disembarked the hovering aircraft and rushed to the crashed helicopter, finding the gun ship's engine still running and fuel leaking from the cells near the loaded rocket pods.

Specialist Whaley entered the cockpit and struggled to shut down the engine for fear that the leaking fuel would ignite and detonate the rockets. Unable to free the jammed fuel controls to shut down the engine. Specialist Whaley, fearing an imminent explosion, dragged the critically injured pilot from the wreckage and carried him to the waiting rescue helicopter for evacuation to Medical facilities. Specialist Five Whaley's heroic actions were in keeping with the highest traditions of the military service and reflect great credit upon himself, his unit, and the United States Army.

Thus were the events of 10 October 1969 for Charlie Whaley, Crew Chief of UH-1H 67-17624 and the rest of the crew- CW2 Billy Woodyard, Aircraft Commander (AC), and Medic David Reeves. The Co-Pilot is unknown. Day 2 of 3 of "Stand-by" at Quang Tri, it was a typical rainy day, but there is more to the story than what is included in the orders above.

**Warrant Officers Jim Harris, left,
Billy Woodyard, right**

A "good ole boy" from North Carolina, Charlie remembers the mission in more detail,

"We had just refueled and were shutting down at the "Glossy Pinner" helipad at Quang Tri. The blades were still turning when this Marine Officer came up to us; I think he may have been a Chaplain.

As the Aircraft Commander was filling out the logbook, this Marine started talking to him and before long, Mr. Woodyard said, 'Let's go, we got some where to go.' The Marine had given us the coordinates and we flew out to those coordinates. When we got there, we all knew we were someplace we weren't supposed to be! The crash site was in the Demilitarized Zone, DMZ. We found the crash site pretty quickly, but strangely there were no other aircraft around, nobody. We could see people down there moving around but we couldn't tell who they were. The gunship had crashed into a ravine and we couldn't land, so I told Mr. Woodyard, 'If you'll bring her down close to the ground, I'll go see what's goin' on.'"

Charlie remembers the crash scene, "We got within about 5 feet of the ground at the top of the ravine and I bailed out. The engine in the crashed helicopter was still screaming at full throttle, even after all this time. The injured pilot was a great big guy and I think he had a broken leg.

Charlie Whaley, 1969, in an old, gray, one-piece flight suit!

The guys in the back were dead as well as the other pilot. The deceased pilot was decapitated when the blades came through the cockpit and it appeared that the door gunners had been thrown from the aircraft and were mashed by the crashing helicopter, a Charlie Model Huey. I was able to bring the engine down to an idle, but that was it. I tried the flight idle detent, the fuel switch and even tried pulling circuit breakers on what was left of the overhead console, but the engine continued to turn. They were fully loaded with rockets and probably fuel; wherever they were going, they didn't get there.

I unbuckled the injured pilot and threw him over my shoulder in a fireman's carry and I started up the hill, but I could not get up the hill because of his weight. So I laid him down, took off my armor and threw him back over my shoulder. Without those extra pounds, I made it back the 30 or 40 feet to the top of the hill.

Our bird came back down and I raised the pilot up enough so that Reeves, the Medic, could get hold of him and we lifted him into the aircraft. We did not use the hoist at all on this mission, just muscle power... And adrenaline!

After he was safely inside the helicopter, I then climbed up on the skid and pulled myself in. As soon as I got plugged back in to the intercom, Mr. Woodyard said, 'God damn, Whaley, that's the bravest thing I've ever seen!'

We went straight to the hospital ship. The pilot was alive and conscious when we got him to the hospital ship. He had regained consciousness during the flight out of the crash area. He had a head injury with a gash in his head. He seemed to know what was going on but we did not have any conversation. To this day, I don't know if he survived. I can only assume that he did.

What was so bad about all this to me was that when we got back to Camp Evans after our standby was over; I got my ass chewed out by Major Hull, the CO, because I lost my armor plate! We didn't have anymore and I had to fly without it. I guess that was my punishment for taking off my chicken plate!"

For some reason, a Soldier's Medal doesn't seem enough for Charlie Whaley on this mission, even though it <u>was</u> for heroism. But better than an Article 15 reprimand for losing his armor, I suppose.

David Reeves, who was present on that mission as Medic, offered the following statement,

"To Whom It May Concern:

The following is my recollection as to those events in which Specialist Charlie Whaley not only distinguished himself well above the standards of any Army Medevac Crew Chief, but his actions also contributed to the overall moral and reflected the true nature of what Dustoff in Vietnam was.

As I recall, following the initial request to search and rescue for a downed helicopter, I remember foremost the mood change on board. The seriousness of the matter was evident listening over the intercom to the voices of Charlie and our Pilots.

Discussion first centered on finding the downed chopper in the jungle with only a general reference as to the location, then how to determine if anyone survived the crash since no ground support was at the site or near the area. After a somewhat lengthy search the craft was identified inverted, smoking and partially visible in the bottom of in a ravine.

Recognizing that there was no visible sign of life as we hovered above the craft, Charlie concurred with the Pilot and requested to go down at his own risk and search the aircraft on the ground. Since hoisting was impractical due to the orientation of our chopper, the pilot gave Charlie the "go ahead." During this I recall warnings from other aircraft above us that enemy combatants were spotted in the area above us and the crash site. Presumably they were also looking for the downed chopper.

So without thought to his own safety, Charlie jumped out and into the brush and worked his way down the steep slope to the smoldering helicopter that was orientated some 20-30 feet or so below and to our left. My attention then was simply to support the pilot in his orientation and keep the blades from striking the side of the hill.

What happened next was unforgettable. Charlie climbed into the downed burning chopper and discovered one seriously injured pilot. And without any assistance carried him back up the slope to our skid where he managed by himself to lift the injured above his head to the doorway where I was could drag the patient on aboard.

As to the nature of the patient's injuries, which appeared grave at the time, I only recall that Charlie was there helping me in treating this patient during the return flight.

Also it should be noted that Charlie never bragged as to how brave his actions were... And they were heroic, that day. During any mission on his tour he always took care of his ship, supported his pilots and especially watched over the Medics.

Thank you Charlie.

David Reeves, Medic."

As the author, I can back up David's claim of, "no bragging." I was in the unit at that time, and flew with Charlie many times after this mission. I never heard him say one word about this rescue, and I didn't even find out about it until doing research for this book years later. Amazing!

One final word about Charlie Whaley. He was transferred to the 237th from the 571st. When he reported to Major Hull, he had all his equipment with him including an M79 grenade launcher, a machine gun of some sort and two or three other weapons that he had "procured". The Major's comment?

"I don't know who you are or where you got all that stuff, but you're flying with me!"

Mission 8

There was no billboard that said "WELCOME TO LAOS"
Steve Woods, Keith Shafer, Jerry Graff and Wayne "Doc Gordie" Gordon

From the 366th Tactical Fighter Wing – Da Nang *Gunfighter Gazette*, Volume V, Number 8, dated December 5, 1970: *By Captain Mike Freel*

"Da Nang may not be everyone's cup of tea, but two 366th Tactical Fighter Wing pilots, Capt. James R. Robinson and 1st Lt. Donald A. Boulet II of the 421st and 390th Tactical Fighter Squadrons, respectively, will positively tell you Da Nang is all right. It beats punching out of an F-4 and spending 4 hours on the ground in hostile territory," said Captain Robinson, who along with his back-seater, Lieutenant Boulet, did just that last Wednesday.

"We punched out at about 1500 feet in a heavy cloud bank," explained Lieutenant Boulet, "which actually was a plus factor because 'Charlie' could not get a fix on us."

The two landed on a ridge about a mile apart in country that was described by Captain Robinson, "as rolling, muddy and full of trails, which you can be sure we both did our best to avoid.

The punch out and the landing was uneventful except I got hung up in a tree about six feet off the ground," continued the captain. The first SAR (Search and Rescue - Ed.) aircraft on the scene were the "Spads" and "Jolly Greens" from Da Nang followed by U.S. Army "Huey" helicopters.

We can't say enough for the rescue people who came to our aid," praised Captain Robinson, "especially the 'Huey' from the 571st U.S. Army Medical Detachment from Quang Tri, piloted by Warrant Officer Woods. Those guys really 'stuck it out' flying back and forth across the terrain trying to get a fix on us.

In fact they took sufficient battle damage on the first try to extract us that they had to recover and return with a second chopper to get us out," added Lieutenant Boulet. "Our sincere thanks to all who participated," said both aviators. "An exciting day," said Captain Robinson, whose 29th birthday was, you guessed it, last Wednesday.

And so it went; that day in 1970, as two more lives were saved by a DUSTOFF crew in South Vietnam. But as our "good friend and newscaster" Paul Harvey says, "And now you'll hear, the *rrrrest* of the story..."

During this period of the Vietnam War, things became so "busy" in Northern I Corps that assets of the 237th Medical Detachment, DMZ DUSTOFF, and the 571st Medical Detachment, Phu Bai DUSTOFF, were often combined to complete missions. Losses to both aircraft and personnel in those two units were so high that crews and aircraft were often "mixed together." This included additional aircraft from other units, including the 498th Medical Detachment, but no other personnel from the 498th, only helicopters.

On this particular mission, Warrant Officer Steven Woods and 1LT Keith O. Shafer were assigned to the 571st while the other crew members on board were from the 237th. The aircraft on this mission was 69-15216, "The Peace Seeker," as the nose art indicated, an aircraft assigned to the 237th and normally flown by Crew Chief Specialist 5 Jerry Graff and Medic Specialist 5 Wayne "Doc Gordie" Gordon.

Crew Chiefs were assigned to perform the daily maintenance of their aircraft and routinely flew each mission on "his" helicopter; there is a certain amount of military wisdom in that theory. "You worked on it, you fly in it!" Jerry Graff was one of the first to become aware of the mission. His description of setting up the aircraft was typical of the missions flown... One never knew what to expect when a mission came in. It was the proverbial "Luck of the Draw!"

Wayne and I had just finished flying first up the day before and we had just switched with the other crew, we had completed our inspections and cleanup of our aircraft. The other crew wanted to get some things done so they had walked off and Wayne and I had gone to the Barracks for some rest and to get cleaned up. The phone rang looking for the other crew because they just received a phone call from the tower at the airfield about a downed F-4 out near the Laos border.

We went to the radio room and started to figure out where to get the crew.

The Crew Chief and Medic had gone over to the airfield for some items they needed and so we decided that we would cover them on the mission and it was decided that I would prepare my aircraft to fly the mission instead of taking their aircraft.

This meant I would have to move the hoist from their aircraft to 216. I moved the gear of the two pilots to my aircraft and moved the hoist to 216. That was no easy task and I ended up damaging my back during the move. When the pilots showed up with all the information the other crews also came back. We decided that since we were ready to go, the two first up pilots went with our aircraft and the other crew would follow us out for a communication link with our control center during the search.

Following is Aircraft Commander Steve Woods' statement:

"At 1000 hrs. On 2 Dec. 1970, I was notified by Lt. Shafer that two Air Force pilots had been shot down about 30 miles southwest of Quang Tri. I assembled an all-volunteer crew to go on the search. I was Aircraft Commander, Lt. Shafer volunteered to fly as pilot and Specialist Graff was the Crew Chief and Specialist Gordon was the Medic.

I instructed the crew to install the hoist and then we departed for the crash site. The weather wasn't very good but it didn't give us much of a problem. I decided to fly low level and instructed the crew to maintain an alert for enemy fire. We arrived in the general area where the crew was shot down and began our search. We drew concentrated enemy fire on several occasions but only got hit once."

1LT Keith O. Shafer:

"While we were on standby at Quang Tri, I got a call from 'Pamper', the radar guys. I was told that a Fox Four (F-4 Air Force Jet) had gone down somewhere along the border. I believe they gave me some general coordinates but they did not have a pinpoint site. We did not realize at the time that we would wind up in Laos.

We had a solid low ceiling somewhere around 500-700 feet but the visibility was OK. As we headed out in the general area, we made contact with 'King' the Air Force Search and Rescue (SAR) Command and Control (C&C) aircraft. 'King' was receiving a beeper signal from one of the downed pilots and tried to give us directions of where to head for our search.

The area was about 35-40 minutes from Quang Tri so we only had about an hour of flight time on site before we would need to head back to refuel. At that time, we were the only ones below the clouds while all of the Air Force was above the cloud layer."

Steve Woods continues:

"We remained on station until we got low on fuel and then returned to Mai Loc. We inspected the aircraft and found only minor damage. We went back to the area and continued the search. A Cobra spotted the parachute of the downed Co-Pilot. My Crew Chief spotted him on the ground. The Medic operated the hoist and lifted him aboard while WO George advised me of my position. We located the pilot about 100 meters to the east and hoisted him aboard also. The performance of the entire crew was outstanding and made the rescue successful. Their determination in the face of enemy fire is indeed a tribute to Army Aviation."

Jerry Graff describes the refueling,

"I found a round had entered the bottom of the tail boom and exited next to the tail rotor shaft cover.

Both holes were in the skin of the aircraft and not any structural part of the aircraft was damaged.

We decided to return to the search area and continue the operation. The Cobra crew said they would work with us and wished the NVA would try something as he still had a full load of ammo!"

Keith Shafer continues:

"After refueling, we made contact with 'King' again and after much back and forth comm (communications) on guard we heard one of the Jolly Green Giant pilots say, 'If they could get the Army out of the way they would get the job done!' Needless to say, this just pissed us off and made us more determined to find the downed pilots.

Steve Woods WO1, Dustoff 509

By this time a Cobra gunship joined us on station so here we are... Two Army helicopters searching the jungle low-level and half the Air Force are above the clouds doing their circle-jerk!"

Keith Shafer LT, Dustoff 507

Warrant Officer Kenneth George was in a second aircraft, supporting Mr. Woods. Mr. George's statement,

"On 2 Dec 1970 I was pilot aboard Dustoff 710. Dustoff 509 received a request to perform a search and rescue mission for two pilots who had been shot down.

Dustoff 710 flew out to Khe Sanh so that we could maintain communications with our sister ship and Dustoff Control. The area of the search was reported to be filled with enemy 37mm gun positions. Dustoff 509 drew concentrated enemy fire on several occasions but was able to make the rescue of the two pilots after 4 hours of search."

(Note: Pilot call signs of the 571st started with "5" and pilot call signs of the 237th started with a "7". Thus, 509, 710, etc. As a 571st pilot, Mr. Woods was 509 and as a 237th pilot, Mr. George was 710.)

And the Cobra gunship… From Captain Joseph F. Keller. We can't overlook his statement:

"On 2 December 1970, I was the escort gunship team leader helping Dustoff 509 to extract two Air Force pilots who had been shot down about 30 miles southwest of Quang Tri. In making the pickup of the two pilots, Dustoff 509 was forced to contour fly low level in order to reduce exposure time.

The area of the pickup site was in the location of a known enemy infiltration route.

On several occasions, Dustoff 509 came under intense automatic weapons fire. Although he took hits in the tail boom of his aircraft, Dustoff 509 continued the mission. Disregarding their own safety, Dustoff 509 continued to search for the downed pilots. After much searching, Dustoff 509 was able to locate and hoist both of the pilots out. Only the skill of the two pilots and the bravery of the crew made the mission a complete success."

Keith Shafer:

"I seem to remember the Cobra spotting the first chute and directing us over it. We hovered around for a little while still looking for the pilot while the Cobra Gunship dared anyone to fire at us. We knew he would watch our backs and blow the hell out of anyone who fired at us. The pilot finally crawled out from a bush and we hoisted him aboard."

Aircraft Commander Woods inspecting The Tail Boom of 216 Upon Return To Quang Tri

Crew Chief Graff's comments:

"Wayne hoisted the pilot up while I kept an eye for the other pilot or others that we figured would be showing up before too long. The pilot was able to give us general direction to where the other pilot was located and after a few moments of hovering and not getting shot out of the sky the other pilot came out of the bushes.

The odd part of this was I know we did not have very much time before we had more than a few others showing up and yet I was trying to tell the pilot to break a dead tree branch off so we could land and pick him up instead of getting him on the hoist and out of the area. Finally we had him on board and flying out of the area at 120 Knots.

I remember the one downed pilot asking Wayne if we could go any faster now that they were on board and the look on his face when he told them this was it, we couldn't go any faster! They told us they were hit by radar controlled guns and they were at 600 knots. They appeared very happy once we were able to place them back at a military base."

After hoisting the second pilot aboard, 1LT Shafer continues:

"We low-leveled our way back to Quang Tri and dropped off the pilots at the Emergency Room of the 18th Surgical Hospital. After shutting down, we inspected the aircraft and found several small arms hits in the tail boom. We then went in and talked to the pilots of 'Stormy 02'. One had a sprained ankle but other than that they were both OK.

They said they really got scared when we were flying tree top level heading back to the hospital!"

In a 1990 letter to Wayne Gordon, Jim Robinson offers more information about how they got shot down and a little bit of background on their mission. Portions of his letter include,

"There were 3 Air Force squadrons at Da Nang, 390th, 421st, 4th, but also a volunteer squadron by the name of 'STORMY' which took people (only volunteers) from the other 3 squadrons for a 3 month tour. The reason it was voluntary and only 3 months was that generally you got your ass shot off. We were a single ship operation doing high speed low level visual recon for targets of opportunity in North Vietnam, Laos and later, Cambodia. We carried no bombs, just a small pod of 'Willy Pete' (White Phosphorus –Ed.) rockets to mark targets and the 20mm cannon because we also had a backup S.A.R. mission.

Don (my GIB from the 390th, I was from the 421st) and I were in 'STORMY' the day you found us wandering around rural Laos lookin' for a motel and a cold beer.

We were just breezin' down the 'Laos Freeway' at about 500 feet and 500 knots when it seems as though we pissed-off some North Vietnam tourist around 'Delta-45'. You know some people just can't take a joke... A little buzz job and they really get irate!!! Well from that point forward my life turned to shit in a hand basket, but quick!

Now, I've been hit before... But, hell, you don't have to blow the whole airplane away to get my attention... I know when I'm not invited! EXIT–one F-4E Phantom Fighter (brand-spankin' new... Less than 400 hours... That pissed the Wing Commander off)... ENTER–one US Army (Who invited these guys!!!) Huey 'Dustoff' chopper!!!

The Air Force is still scratchin' their head how you got involved... But to Don and I it could have been the Lone Ranger, Batman and his queer sidekick Robin or Three Fiddlers Fiddling... You looked like the 'Great White Knight' to us with two tickets out of Laos-land and totally incorrigible company!!! Cleanin' up their rice-paddies (at the very best... Not likely) or being face down in a pool of my own blood (more likely than not) was not my idea of "career advancement"!!! Needless to say... Thanks once again."

Wayne Gordon replied to Captain Robinson's letter; here is an excerpt from it:

"*While we were getting the coordinates and checking all of our equipment… They gave us encouragement by saying we'll give you all the protection you need… Just get our men out! Our ship crossed the border into Laos and proceeded to your approximate position… Which looked like a Kennedy Airport air show… There were so many different kinds of aircraft looking for you guys… We went into a valley at treetop level, went up the crest of a hill when the jungle below us opened up… Mr. Woods did a 180 and went top end speed trimming trees to get out of range; we thought we saw something below…*

Being low on fuel, we left and went back to Vietnam to refuel and assess the damage at Mai Loc… Jerry said it was not structural… Took a vote if we should go back… We all said, 'Let's go'… Off we went to get you guys out… A lot of things were in your favor… You had the best Pilots in our Units. Jerry knew what the ship was able to withstand… And having a Medic who did HOT HOIST before…

"Doc Gordie" Wayne Gordon, Medic

Not to mention that we usually don't carry the Hoist on board unless requested... So with all these in order and a little luck we should be able to get you out! And thank God it worked!

After our flight back to Quang Tri, 18ᵗʰ Surgical Hospital, an Army Officer balled us out for violating another country's airspace... Your Commander praised us and said we were going to get a medal for our action... The Army Officer told us not to accept it, that the Army was going to give it to us.

Jerry Graff, Crew Chief

Isn't that a kick in the ass... Here we are saving two American asses and we got balled out... That's the Army for ya!"

Doc Gordie remembered the flight back to the 18th Surg. as an incredible sight. "There must have been 50 aircraft in a V-formation following us back to Quang Tri!" Unfortunately, no known photo of that formation exists, but it had to have been an incredible hodge-podge of Army and Air Force aircraft escorting Dustoff 509 home. Soon after the rescue, a party was thrown in Da Nang by the Air Force's 366th Tactical Fighter Wing for the crew of Dustoff 509.

Doc Gordie continues his letter to Robinson with this recollection:

"The party was hard to forget... You guys had a Hall filled with food that us Army Fly Boys don't see! Roast Beef, Turkey, Potatoes, Jello, Salads and only God knows what else... The Champaign we had to chug-a-lug (which I haven't touched since that time)... The wheel-barrow with the gold balls that were hung on our zippers by a Lady in a flight suit...

Saying we had BRASS BALLS... Your Commanding Officer stood up on stage... Rose his arms into the air over his head... You guys stood at attention with your glasses toasting him and saying... 'HIM... HIM... F***K HIM'... Then proceeded to throw food and junk at him until he lowered his arms... Then you all sat down with respect! It was unbelievable...

Air Force pilots are too much... I don't remember much about that day except HUG-GING your FLUSHED TOILET and meeting RRRRRRRAALPH!!!, AND YOUR FALCONS... And the most interestin' flight back to Phu Bai in our DRUNKIN' HAZE... I still don't know how we got back, we wobbled and rocked back and forth in the air and had one of our roughest landings ever!!! But worth every minute of it."

Keith Shafer remembers a little more detail:

"That was the best party I have ever been to. I remember our whole crew going through a receiving line of all the fighter wing pilots to include the Jolly Green pilots. When Woody asked which one said he wanted us to get out of the way so they could get the job done, the guilty party was identified. He offered us a ride in his 'real helicopter' and Woody told him, 'If you ain't Dustoff, you ain't shit - come ride with us and we will show you what it's like to be a real pilot!' I remember the Wing Commander saying, 'You give'em Hell, Woody!' And slapped him on the back. Yes, we did get some medals but I think all of us were rewarded with the idea of saving two guys from capture and have had the pleasure of being proud of that for the rest of our lives."

So there it is, one mission in the tapestry of Dustoff in Vietnam. Note that most every-one says "about 30 miles southwest of Quang Tri"… Never "into Laos." Why is that impor-tant?

While the Air Force celebrated the Dustoff crew's rescue of the two F-4 pilots with a "Major League" party, the Army wanted to Court Martial them for flying into Laos! It was OK for the bad guys to violate Laos, but not us! What's up with that?

Doc Gordie's statement during the interview for this story, I think, says it best, *"We were flying off our maps and there was no billboard that said, 'Welcome to Laos!'"*

The crewmembers of Dustoff 509 were all put in for the DFC, Distinguished Flying Cross, one of the highest awards a Dustoff crewmember could hope to achieve. However, as it seems with most Dustoff award recommendations, they were downgraded. Instead of DFC's, they were all awarded Air Medals with "V" device for Valor, still a prestigious recog-nition of their actions.

Considering they were almost given a Court Martial for this mission, one would suppose they should be damned happy they didn't lose their wings!"

"And now you know, the rrrrest of the story! Paul Harvey, Good Day!"

Mission 9

7000 Feet

Like most war stories, "There I was, 7000 feet…" But I'm getting ahead of myself.

It was 1969, a year that some consider was the height of the Vietnam War. I was a Medevac helicopter pilot, a Warrant Officer 1, with only 2 months of combat experience "under my holster" when this mission unfolded. My holster being a "John Waynish" gun belt that held a 5 shot military issue .38 pistol and about 20 rounds of extra ammunition. Of course, if we ever had to use it, it would probably only urinate off the enemy or perhaps he would die (or seriously injure himself) laughing from the folly of me firing it. However, many of us claimed that should the need arise, we would save the last round for ourselves rather than become a prisoner of the dreaded Viet Cong or North Vietnamese Army, either one. Whether we would have actually done so or not will probably be argued for eternity…

Regarding the mission that this narrative documents, we did find ourselves at 7000 feet in the mountains. I was flying with our Commanding Officer, Major Donald R. Hull.

He was a pilot who probably did not have to fly because of his position, but always took his turn at the stick. Regardless of the mission, if his name came up in the rotation, he flew. In fact, two months later on a night when I was wounded and our ship was damaged, he put together a crew and took over for us in very hostile territory. He had less than 2 weeks left in country, and very easily could have assigned someone else to fly the coverage, but he didn't. I have always admired him for that... He truly was a leader. The night of this mission, he again displayed his abilities to command others.

Major Donald Hull, at right, original 237th Commanding Officer, demonstrating the hoist and the Stokes Litter to the crews. Dan Fanelli at left in cargo compartment, Charlie Whaley Crew Chief sitting on cargo floor. AC 67-17624.

On September 12, the 7000 foot mission came in an hour or two after darkness had set in, and in Vietnam, an "unindustrialized" nation, there were very few lights, if any, more than a quarter mile or so from the main roads. Because of this, flying in the mountains could be very dangerous; there were absolutely no references to the ground and no way to know exactly where we were. Navigation at night in VN was *very* primitive in a Huey. On a moonless night, we often could not even see the mountaintops; I dreaded flying in the mountains in the dark, as there were many documented helicopter crashes at night into hillsides. Look as hard as you want, you won't see the horizon; sometimes, my mind would see mountaintops that weren't there.

On this night, we headed due west from Camp Evans to pick up a wounded GI with a head wound. We knew we would be in "Charlie Country" because of the location of the coordinates we were given. It was not going to be a short flight... And bad weather was rolling in.

Within a very few minutes after breaking ground, we started encountering clouds.

Even at the distance we were from the Landing Zone (LZ), we were able to contact the troops on the ground via our FM radio and they assured us they could see stars. With that information, Maj. Hull began to climb over the cloud layer, both of us confident that we would be able to complete the mission on the other side of the cloudbank. In addition, climbing higher allowed us to fly without worry of inadvertent and intimate contact with mountaintops. We did NOT want to try flying under the clouds in the mountains.

As we continued west, we found ourselves also continuing to climb higher to stay over the cloud tops. The common theory that we flew with was that as long as we were at least 1500 feet above the ground, we were out of range of small arms fire; above 1500 feet (and below 50 feet) was out of "The Dead Man's Zone." But this was getting ridiculous; we hardly EVER flew this high on a mission. At about 5000 feet, the Major called the guys on the ground again. "Yep, we can still see the stars." So we flew on... Wondering if they were lying to us, just to get us to come in, regardless of the weather.

At 7000 feet, we were still clear of the cloud tops and felt that we were very close to the LZ, but we were still looking at solid clouds! Another call to the pickup site... "We can hear you, our strobe light is out." Here we are, 100 knots and looking down at a solid cloud layer, over the pickup site; NOW what do we do? I peered through my clear helmet visor, down into the clouds out my door, wondering how we were going to rescue this injured grunt, when a flash caught my eye. It was a strobe light, several thousand feet down in a darker than a sack full of assholes mountain valley, and the light was coming up through a very small hole in the clouds.

"Sir, I can see their strobe through a hole in the clouds." Immediately, Major Hull said, "You've got it!" I couldn't believe it... Here I was a junior pilot flying with the most senior pilot in the unit on a very dangerous mission, and he's giving me the aircraft! Without hesitation, I took over the controls and bottomed the pitch, beginning a spiral descent through the hole and trying to keep the strobe light in sight all the way down. I knew that if I stayed in sight of the light, I would be clear of obstructions and also not lose their position. Besides, if I flew into the clouds, it could result in tragic consequences; i.e. vertigo or mountain tops.

Quite often, the guys on the ground would put their strobe light in their helmet, then "aim" their open helmet into the sky towards the approaching helicopter. By doing this, any enemy on the ground would have difficulty seeing the strobe but the helicopter crew could readily see it from altitude. Only very recently did this author learn that some of the troops on the ground took this procedure one step further. They dropped their strobe light into the muzzle of their M79 grenade launcher, a very large bore weapon, to *thoroughly* insure no one on the ground could see the light as the weapon barrel was pointed towards us. Yet we, as helicopter crews flying at night with no ground references, were supposed to land with the enemy that close... So close that the good guys were worried that the bad guys might see them. We landed to those concealed lights on a regular basis.

Our normal procedure on the nighttime landings was to black out the helicopter during final approach. All external lights were turned off, and we would even turn off the overhead console and instrument panel lights so they could not be seen from the ground.

As we got very near the ground and the Landing Zone, we would finally turn on the landing light so that we could see exactly where we were going to set the aircraft down. The landing light would be turned off the moment we touched down.

On one occasion, we were going in to pick up a wounded POW who had tried to penetrate a perimeter of tanks at night. I was just touching down in tall grass when the Medic yelled, "Pull up, we just landed on someone!" Afraid we had just landed on one of the tankers giving us cover, I keyed the microphone to the radio operator on the ground, "I think we just landed on one of your men!" He immediately replied, "Nah, that's one of the sappers that tried to get in, he's already dead."

Back to the mission at hand, as we continued to descend through the hole, I don't remember the altimeter reading as we flew past the bottoms of the clouds, but what I do recall is that the moment we were in the clear, all the windows fogged up! Going from the cooler high altitude, into the warm and damp valley, was something I had never en-countered and we were in trouble!

Major Hull turned on the bleed air (defroster) to clear the windshield, but as in an automobile, it doesn't happen right away! Luckily, my door window was open, and I was able to SOMEWHAT look out the side window to continue flying, but really could only barely see forward with one eye and still hold on to the controls. It was quite a stretch, but now my concern was that I seemed to be several thousand yards away from the strobe light in the LZ and no idea where the mountainsides were. I told the guys in the back to keep an eye out for the ground and valley walls, but because of the darkness, they were as blind as I was because of the foggy windshield. As we high hovered up the valley, we were the proverbial "sitting ducks." Why we took no fire from the enemy, I'll never know; at least I saw no tracers coming up at us. The bad guys were down there; they had just shot this guy, and we were coming in to pick him up.

I continued to press on in the direction that I had last seen the strobe, and as we closed in on the LZ, the windshield finally cleared enough to see out the front of the helicopter. Had it not cleared when it did, things could have gotten very dangerous for us. I had never tried to land a helicopter with my head hanging out the side window, but this time we got lucky.

As we touched down, I was pleasantly surprised that the Major had allowed me to complete the landing; I was pleased that he had enough confidence in me to allow me to continue the flight and I was *also* pleasantly surprised that we hadn't crashed! As the Medic and Crew Chief loaded our patient, I took a quick look out my side window and up into a tiny hole in the clouds; it was the one we had just dropped through. I then keyed my intercom and said to Major Hull "Sir, they weren't lying, I can see stars." I don't remember his reply, but I'm certain he had an incredulous smile on his face, even though I couldn't see it.

Seconds later, we were lifting off, me still on the controls and clawing our way back up through that same hole. As a matter of procedure, we always told the ground troops to which hospital we were taking the wounded. Normally we waited for the Medic to advise where to take the injured, but knowing our grunt had a head injury, we were able to quickly tell the radio operator on the ground that we were taking him to the Navy hospital ship. His reply made my whole time in country worth the risk and effort necessary, "Thanks a HELL of a lot, Dustoff!"

The heartfelt emotion of his reply came through in his voice; from the sound and the tone of it, I would guess that the injured soldier was a very good friend of his. It was the proverbial "warm fuzzy" to know we were appreciated for taking such a risk.

I'm not sure who landed at the hospital ship that night, probably Major Hull, but I have never forgotten this as my second most memorable mission in country. Most of all, I appreciated the confidence Don Hull had in me to allow me to take over the rescue when he did. There would have been no questions asked had he taken back the controls at any time. Many years after this event, I asked him about the mission and why he gave me the controls when he did. "Hell, I couldn't see anything!" was his reply. And as to why he didn't take the controls back once things got really "hairy?" "You were doing fine" or words to that effect was his answer. Regardless, he was still boosting my confidence, even now. And I believe that mission helped convince him to later promote me to Aircraft Commander over others who had more time in country than I.

Finally, some time after we landed back at Evans and knowing that I was the unit Awards Officer responsible for submitting paperwork for medals, the Major looked at me and said, "You know, we ought to get a medal or something for that one!" Of course, the next day I got right on it, and forwarded the paperwork through "channels."

Nothing was ever heard from Headquarters regarding the medals, and frankly, I would have been pleasantly surprised if we had. A few years ago, there was an article in *Reader's Digest* about an Air Force pilot who flew his C-123 (I think) onto a runway in Vietnam that was under fire and rescued 3 or 4 guys on the ground.

The article extolled his bravery and heroism for this mission on which he received a glorious medal for his actions. I showed the article to my wife and facetiously told her what an "amazing" story it was... And then I reminded her that what he did was a "piece of cake" compared to what we did virtually every day as Dustoff crews.

Am I bitter about that? Absolutely not. I know what we did and couldn't be more proud of the fact that I had the privilege and opportunity to be a Dustoff pilot.

I know what we did as Dustoff crews...
And the guys we picked up know what we did.
That's plenty good enough for me...

Thank you Major Hull... For allowing me
to become a man.

Mission 10

Dave Acreman's Reply To 7000 Feet

When I wrote the story "7000 Feet," I could not remember who the guys in the back were... I still don't know. Following is a reply I received from one of our Medics,

"Mr. Marshall,

I read the story "7000 Feet" and I re-member a lot of night missions just as scary. One that I remember was a daytime Mission with Capt. Colvin. We landed in a hot LZ to pick up three litter patients and some ambu-latory. As soon as we touched down he began to count to ten. He had stated beforehand, if we weren't in the Chopper when he said ten we were going to get left. Just as he said, "seven" both crewmembers (Ortega and me) yelled, "CLEAR" and we pulled up.

John Colvin CPT. at rear.
David Tousignant 1LT nearest camera.

After reaching approximately treetop
level, a mortar round hit where we had been
and a fragment of shrapnel cracked the chin
bubble of the aircraft. I'm glad he counted,
and we were racing against the count. I am
looking at my flight time log as was recorded on Form DA 759-1 for the month in
question for you, and I flew 0.8 hrs on Sept
11th and 4.4 hrs on Sept 13th. If the date of
Sept 12th is correct, I guess you can rule me
out as the Medic on the 7000-foot mission. I
hope you find the rest of the crew, as Paul
Harvey says, "The rest of the Story."

**David "Ace" Acreman Medic
DMZ Dustoff Medic 68-69**

Mission 11

Crew Chief Doc Halliday
Flying At Night In Bad Weather

During the Vietnam War, Army helicopter crews and the Infantryman on the ground suffered a higher casualty rate then any other class of Vietnam soldier. However, unlike the "ground pounders" helicopters suffered a very high accident rate. These losses were due not only to pilot error, but also to an occasional mechanical failure and quite a few to bad weather, especially at night. In fact, only about 50% of helicopter crew and aircraft losses were due to combat; the other half was due to "other than combat."

The 237th Medical Detachment, DMZ Dustoff, was typical in this regard. Officially, 15 men in the 237th were Killed In Action, KIA, during the war. Of the 15 men lost, 7 were pilots and 8 were Medics or Crew Chiefs. Eight men were lost due to "accident" the other 7 due to hostile fire. (On a side note, while there are no confirmed numbers, pilots and crewmembers also suffered equally from wounds, Wounded In Action, WIA, due to enemy fire). *Every one* of the 8 men from the 237th lost in accidents was due to bad weather at night.

It can be argued that many of the accidents that occurred were at least partially caused by the youth and inexperience of the Army helicopter pilot. Many Army pilots enlisted for flight school right out of High School. Because of this ability to enlist (specifically to fly) at such a young age, after the required year of training, many found themselves flying helicopters in Vietnam at the age of 19. Most pilots were not much older than 20 or 21, but by the time they were promoted to Aircraft Commander, AC, they had hundreds of hours of combat experience, flying hundreds of missions on an almost daily basis. Perhaps some felt it not necessary or inconvenient to practice instrument flying, but they were good aviators! VERY good! And, yes, some made fatal mistakes, also.

This narrative, however, is focused only on the losses of the 237th and should be quite typical of the harrowing missions of the Dustoff Hueys and their crews. DMZ Dustoff Crew Chief Dan "Doc" Halliday remembers two of those missions well.

Dan was the Crew Chief of a UH-1H Huey, serial number 70-15805, which Dan nicknamed "Right Here, Buddy."

"I stenciled it on the nose above the red cross after my very first mission when I saw the face of the first grunt I picked up.   I thought it was appropriate." After the first mission with the new nose art, Dan decided that "Here's Your Buddy" was more appropriate, so the change was made and stayed that way for some time. Flying out of Lane Army Airfield at An Khe, Dan remembers a mission shortly before Christmas of 1971, when they were called out about 2 in the morning for a mission. From a "satellite" site near Tuy Hoa on the coast, they took off and headed to the pickup site.   Aircraft Commander 1LT Phil Roby and copilot WO1 Kenneth George decided the Landing Zone (LZ) was too "socked in" to safely try an approach... They could not see the ground to land and looking back, it was probably a very wise decision not to go any further with the mission.

Dan "Doc" Halliday Relaxing In His Hooch

But now, they had to return to base. They decided to go "feet wet" flying out over the ocean and then homing in on Tuy Hoa. No high obstacles to worry about over the ocean, just a little fog. A couple miles out and feeling relatively safe as they turned towards "home" they saw what appeared to be a Surface to Air Missile (SAM) fired at them! The pilots dove for the water to try to evade the missile and successfully did so, but they now found themselves in the fog. Climbing to 500 feet, and still in the fog, the pilot on the controls began to get vertigo and started descending again, this time in a spiral in order to try to find a place to land.

Dan then saw white sand from the beach blowing up from the rotor wash and alerted the pilots, who then immediately started a climb to altitude again.

Dan felt this latest maneuver to be so steep that damage to the aircraft might occur, but apparently, no damage was done. "I was afraid the tail boom would shear off, it was so steep!" Dan recalled. Finally, they were again able to gain altitude and flew down the coast, contacting Tuy Hoa by radio and got back in, "safe and (somewhat?) sound." Dan stated that other than getting shot at on missions, "This one scared me the most!"

When asked about other "memorable" missions, Dan related the pick-up in II Corps about 2 or 3 in the morning, again this time with Phil Roby in command. After a lengthy flight out to the LZ; which was under fire, they approached from the North with Cobra gunships providing cover. As the aircraft touched down, both Dan and Medic George Shaughnessy began picking up patients and loading them onto the aircraft. Dan remembers George running around the nose of the aircraft as he tripped and fell as they were taking fire the entire time. No one was injured further, however the hydraulics were damaged with one small arms round.

Dan related that often, bullet holes were repaired with Coke cans. The crew was recommended for Distinguished Flying Crosses (DFCs) for this mission, however they received "lesser" Air Medals instead for their actions.

And speaking of mistakes, a final question was asked of Dan if he had any other missions he cared to share. Recalling a particularly bad crash scene, he spoke of an "Air Force guy" who went for a joy ride on a test flight in a Huey. They crashed and burned. "That's all I want to say about that one."

Flying Medevac missions at night in marginal weather was bad enough… No need to "tempt fate" any more than that.

Mission 12

Crew Chief And Nurse #8

It was probably October of 1969, or maybe it was one month either way, it doesn't really matter. In Vietnam, being near a "round eye" woman was a rare experience. The local Vietnamese ladies were kind and helpful, but there was nothing like a round eye (an American woman) when one was so far from the "Real World" good 'ole US of A. However, as a Dustoff unit, the 237th Medical Detachment was assigned to a Hospital for Administrative and other support, and we had the luxury of being around the nurses on a daily basis. Our support at DMZ Dustoff at Camp Evans and Quang Tri was the 18th Surgical Hospital and the nurses assigned there were "our" ladies. They were treated with respect and of course, part of the Officers Club, which we all shared. For the most part they were treated like sisters and treated like the professionals that they were. In fact, I know of at least 3 marriages that came out of that blend, all of which still flourish today, but I digress...

The 477th Aerial Rocket Artillery (ARA) based at Camp Evans in 1969 was our "gun cover."

Normally, if we needed gun support on a hot mission, we called for the "Griffins," the call sign of the 477th. But on this night, the Griffins called on us. A party was laid on for them, and even if I knew the "excuse" for the party, I have long forgotten it. But they needed someone to fly out to the Hospital ship in a Huey to bring 7 or 8 Navy nurses from the ship that had accepted the invitation to attend this soiree'.

The Griffins were a unit of the 101st Airborne Division, and were made up entirely of Cobra gunships. Two pilots and thousands of pounds of rompin', stompin' death and destruction... But not one place to put a passenger inside the ship. Many Hueys were available to them, but rarely did those crews make approaches and landings to the Navy Hospital ships Repose or Sanctuary, especially at night! So the call was made to the 237th and without hesitation, the mission was laid on.

Purely by luck of the draw, I was Co-Pilot of the "First Up' ship that night with one of the finest pilots I have ever flown with, Warrant Officer George Zuvela. Like most Warrant helicopter pilots in VN, he flew the missions with gusto and a dash of bravado.

He was an experienced combat pilot and was certainly very proud of that fact. While I don't recall the Medics name that night, I certainly will never forget the Crew Chief... But more on that as the story continues.

USS Sanctuary off the coast of Northern I Corps, where we made many, many landings day and night. We also utilized the USS Repose, a virtually identical ship, with the 2 ships changing stations from Da Nang Harbor about once a week. They always treated us Dustoff guys like royalty and they often listened in on our rescue missions over the FM radios.

The flight out before dark was very routine; we landed on the pitching deck of the ship and waited for our "cargo" to be loaded.

Eight of the loveliest nurses the Navy had to offer; and I mean that sincerely, were about to embark on what was probably their first ride in an Army Huey, and almost certainly their first steps on Southeast Asian terra firma. With everyone strapped in, a normal take-off was completed and we were soon winging our way due south back to Camp Evans.

While it was not an attempt to frighten the ladies, we almost always flew with the cargo doors open and I am sure that the nurses sitting next to those open doors got quite a thrill on the ride in alone! After all, it WAS hot out and we've got this great big fan over our heads and why not take advantage of it? But with us pilots being the "swave and de-boner" guys that we were, George had an idea and I was all for it. Nothing was said, but I could see what he was doing. By kicking in a little bit of pedal, it caused the aircraft to fly out of "trim" and created quite a swirling effect in the cargo compartment with the doors pinned back… Right where 8 nurses were sitting. Gee, what a coincidence! And of course, with the Medic and Crew Chief sitting in their normal places on the cargo floor behind our armored seats, facing backwards, they would have a great view of the ladies trying to keep their skirts from flying up!

Of course, an occasional glance back by the pilots to insure passenger safety was in order, also.

Now one has to understand that we would NEVER do that to OUR nurses, but this was different! This alone should have been a well-deserved reward for ANY red blooded American guy in the back, but it gets better...

The nurse in charge on the flight to the party confirmed the pick up time with George after we landed near the 477th Officer's club. Our arrival was probably around 8 o'clock or so and the bewitching hour was set at 11 or maybe even midnight. Head nurse was assured that even if we were on another mission, someone, another pumpkin, would arrive to take them home from the Ball.

At the appointed hour, we landed back at the coordinates from earlier that evening, the Officer's Club. Idling there, we watched 7 slightly inebriated; some more slightly than others, nurses climb into our aircraft, most with the humble assistance of the swave and de-boner also slightly inebriated gun pilots they had just met at the party. But wait, weren't there 8 nurses on the way over? Aren't we missing one? Head nurse is looking around with a worried expression on her face...

But number 8 is nowhere around. Some of the gunnies head back to the club to look for her... And a few minutes later she finally shows up, hanging on the arm of her newly found best friend. Proper decorum will not allow me to divulge where she was found, but when she finally got to our aircraft, it was obvious from her smile that she had a very good time at the party! Nurse number 8 was put in the hellhole of our "H Model" Huey, one of only two vacant seats left for the flight back.

Because it was now cooler outside, the cargo doors were pulled closed and however it worked out, by chance or by spur of the moment decision, Subject Crew Chief now found himself sitting in the hellhole with Nurse Number 8. Whether by luck or design, he was now trapped with her in the very back of a very noisy helicopter.

The flight to the South China Sea was usually about 15 or 20 minutes from Evans as I remember, and this flight should have been no different. But about 5 minutes into the flight, I hear Subject Crew Chief (SCC) on the intercom, and I can still hear his voice like it was yesterday... "Uh, Sir, uh, this nurse is getting a little friendly with me back here."

I couldn't believe what I was hearing, but George and I just looked at each other and got big grins on our faces. While I don't recall George's exact answer to SCC, it was basically a "Roger that" and the flight continued.

A few minutes later, there was another call on the intercom, "Sir, she's REALLY getting friendly back here, I'd like to take my helmet off for a while if it's OK?" Another reply from George was something like "Go for it!" and I noticed that George had slowed the aircraft down from our normal 100 knots to 80 or so knots. Another big grin on my face, and a sly one on his.

Soon, we're about to go feet wet, crossing the coast to fly out over the Sea. But without saying a word, George begins a slow, almost imperceptible, turn to fly up the coast, rather than heading out to the ship. Grin number 3 crosses my face. Again without saying a word, I know exactly what George is doing. A few minutes later, a gentle 180 turn to fly back down the coast. Oh, by the way, nary a sound out of SCC since he removed his helmet. By now, the trip back is taking twice as long as the trip ashore, and Head Nurse is beginning to suspicion something is amiss.

With the Medic sitting in front of her being the only one she can communicate with, she asks him if there is a problem. "Sir, this Nurse back here wants to know if there is a problem?" George says to tell her something about holding for traffic and we would be landing shortly. This seemed to appease Head Nurse as George then decided it was probably time to take the ladies on home and we again headed due North to the Hospital Ship.

Another uneventful landing on the Hospital ship and the ladies all waved and thanked us for the ride as they walked or... Stumbled across the postage stamp sized landing pad, laughing and grinning all the way. Even Head Nurse smiled and waved. I have no idea if she ever figured out what went on.

For one, all too brief moment, one of my guys in the back had a VERY memorable and VERY enjoyable experience in the back of a Huey. A small reward for a guy who depended totally on us kids in the front, virtually on a daily basis. A guy in the back who literally followed us pilots into harms way on every pickup, literally risking his "life and limb" to save his fellow man and never once refusing to go, regardless of the situation or danger involved.

I never did discuss that night with Subject Crew Chief while we were in Vietnam or even the one time I saw him years later, even though I could pick up the telephone right now and ask him about it. I do remember an intercom, "Thank you" after we took off from the ship, however. In fact, he probably doesn't even remember it was me up front that night, but I'm SURE he remembers George and the "gift" he received from his Aircraft Commander. Maybe I'll ask a couple of the other Crew Chiefs, Charlie Echos, if he ever shared the details of that "hot mission" that night. Or maybe I'll just wait until the next time I see him without his wife and ask him if he ever shared the story with HER! Can you say "Blackmail?" I thought you could!

P.S. I did finally call him and asked him about this story; I can now identify the Crew Chief as Lou Ortega... He told me his wife wouldn't mind. I never could Blackmail anyone, anyway... Dang!

Crew Chief Lou Ortega, Pilot Lee Wood
Medic Al Jenkins, Aircraft 67-17671

Mission 13

Final Flight Of "Curious Yellow"

UH-1H Huey helicopter 69-16656 was assigned to the 237th in March of 1970 and assigned to Crew Chief Specialist Eddie Hopper. For whatever reason which he has yet to explain, Eddie decided to paint the normally flat black nose of the aircraft a bright "school bus" yellow and inscribe the words "Curious Yellow" on it. "Curious Yellow" being the title of a movie that we shall state here as being rated as "Not For Children." Not at all!

Following is a transcript of a presentation given by Warrant Officer Pilot Dave Hansen, DMZ Dustoff 702, on August 8, 2010, at a bi-annual reunion in Indianapolis, Indiana. The patient who is the center of the story, Roger Hill, told the story of his rescue many times to friends and family. His nephew, Bobby Hill, a police forensic artist, took it upon himself to find the crew of the Medevac that saved his uncle's life. Searching the web, he came across the DMZ Dustoff web site, DmzDustoff.org and found the clue he was looking for.

Roger put it this way, "For 25 or 30 years, I told my nephew the aircraft was called, 'Mellow Yellow.'" When Doc Gordie (Medic Wayne Gordon) was eventually contacted to name the crew, Bobby Hill kept insisting the aircraft was called, "Mellow Yellow" when Doc Gordie knew it was "Curious Yellow." Doc says, "We argued back and forth via email. I kept saying it was 'Curious Yellow.'" "No, You don't understand," Bobby finally replied with emphasis, "my uncle *said* the name of the helicopter was "Mellow Yellow." "No, let me tell you" Doc said, "your uncle was wounded and he saw this God coming down with a yellow front and it was really 'Curious Yellow.'" "Are you kidding me?" "No, I'm dead serious, we know the crew and we know what happened that day."

So with that background, we begin the story of "The Final Flight of Curious Yellow." Let's start with the cast of characters as they introduced themselves at the reunion:

"My name is George Shaughnessy, I was in the 237th from 70 to 71 and I have selective amnesia about Vietnam. We were telling some stories earlier and I can't believe we did that stuff!"

"My name is Roger Hill and this is my wife Georgia. I went to Vietnam in 1970 where I was attached to the 5th Special Forces in II Corps at an aide camp and I served with Command & Control North out of Da Nang. I took up residence on hill 950 near Khe Sanh at the end of April, early May and the NVA evicted me in early June. I was wounded pretty badly and Dave Hansen and the crew of Curious Yellow saved my life; and in the process he tried to take my life. I told Dave yesterday that I was made aware by the Veterans Administration that I received my third purple heart because of him.

I got my first one when I got wounded in the aide camp near the Cambodian border just west of Ban Me Thout. The second one was when I got a piece of a Chicom (Chinese Communist) Claymore Mine on Hill 950. Dave wanted to bounce my head down the old Khe Sanh runway a few times for my third one. For a long, long time, over 40 years, I've been wondering who the person was that was carrying a Thompson submachine gun."

Crew Chief Richard Villa, "No, No they didn't do that!" (Grinning)

Roger to George Shaughnessy, "Did you have a submachine gun?" "Actually I had a Thompson, Eddie Iacobacci said I had a .60 caliber machine gun. We had both." (Author's note: Eddie Hopper carried the Thompson.)

Roger, "I was a Special Forces weapons expert and I knew the capabilities of the Thompson submachine gun and it was not a good aircraft weapon. If you wanted to hit anything on the ground you did not want to carry a Thompson. And when I got in that Dustoff I looked at a man carrying a Thompson who wasn't actually carrying one apparently and I thought to myself I had a CAR15, a small version of an M16. I was gonna give it to Eddie because I thought he was gonna be needing it. But then Dave decided to take us down to the valley floor. I apologize if I was rude to anybody. God bless the 237th."

"My name is Dave Hansen and this is my wife Carol, a fantastic lady whom I'm glad can be with me here tonight. I joined the 237th in November of 1970."

With apologies to Dave Hansen for not recording the first minute or two of his Power Point presentation, his transcript follows.

He is already speaking of George Shaughnessy, "We all knew it was gonna be kind of bad but George just jumped right on with his machine gun." (Author's note: George did not have to fly, he simply volunteered with no one asking him to go, knowing that he might be needed.) "The helicopter was virtually new, a very low hour helicopter. You could still smell the fresh paint in that thing, it was a nice machine. This is the crew, this was taken right around June 4, 1971, Ed Iacobacci on the left and Eddie Hopper on the right.

To give you a little bit of Prologue, many of you here were part of the Operation Lam Son 719, the heaviest action I think most of us personally saw.

But the air was just filled with aircraft there at the time. That airstrip at Khe Sanh was just a chaotic mess. There were Army and Air Force aircraft taking off and landing all the time and enemy incoming rounds all the time. The 237th DMZ Dustoff was billeted out there in the dirt at Khe Sanh, we dug these little holes to sleep in and we had these 4-foot corrugated steel culverts sections that was the roof and we slept on stretchers. That was our little compound and it rained half the time and basically it was pretty miserable. The NVA controlled that whole area. They always had and they were always going to. It was the kind of an area that they were in control of; we had made this "little incursion" into their territory.

Here's Gene George with his trusty .38 at his side. He and Alan Rhodes are filling up sand bags; we had to do our own protection.

This slide is a typical mission; I wish I could see closer to see the tail number. We had 2 ships that came up from the 498th Medical Detachment during that time and one of them might even have been 369." (This is in reference to American Huey 369, a Huey that those attending the reunion had a chance to fly the day before. 70-16369 flew in the 498th during this time period.)

See **AmericanHuey369.com**

"Gene George and I were speculating about that possibility and this I believe was one of their ships.

We wondered about the possibility that it might have been. We would go out and make these pickups in Laos and then bring them in to Khe Sanh. We had this kind of a little triage, first aid bunker; sort of under ground with the sand bags around for the doctors so they could figure out what to do with the wounded but here was a typical mission coming in.

Here's the guys taking them over to triage. This kind of reflects what the scene was around there while we had some influence about the area.

What happened after this operation was over was the North Vietnamese Army, NVA, just took over again. They were back in charge except for Roger Hill and his guys. These crazy guys; you see these hills in the background, that's 950 on the left, worn away, and 1015 on the right.

Roger and his group with the Bru Strikers were up there surrounded totally by the NVA regulars and these weren't just little Viet Cong guys running around in black pajamas, these were regular Divisions with Regiments. The area was a very important part of the Ho Chi Minh Trail. It had a lot of branches but there was one place that they had to cross a shallow part of the river that was a bottleneck and that was part of Lam Son 719; it was to cut that off. So the NVA had to stay to control that area that was their weak spot. Roger and his guys were up on this hill all by themselves completely surrounded all the time."

(950 was a state of the art listening post that was using highly classified electronics. If they were ever overrun, their instructions were to blow up the equipment. Explosive charges were pre-set around the receivers. Ed.)

David Tousignant, Pilot, "How many men were with you Roger?"

"I was up there with 2 other Americans that were with me and 46 montagnards. We had a regiment of NVA, attacking us, about 700 NVA."

Dave, "This is what it was like for them up there, they were up high and had a good view, only the view they had was a view of all these guys that wanted to kill 'em! It was pretty wild.

The guy leaning on the sandbags is John Jones, he was the last man killed on 950 in that attack."

Phil Marshall, "The hill in the background is 1015, there is a saddle between 950 and 1015, a low part of the ridgeline."

Roger, "We were taking direct fire down from above on top of there."

Dave, "So the NVA controlled 1015 at that point, right?" "It was a pretty precarious situation. So you were on 950 and they were on the higher ground."

"Here's Dustoff 702, this is Milt Kreger on the left, he was a relatively new pilot, I think he was only with the unit a month or so, not very long. He was pretty much a Newbie, he was kind of hands off at the time, as were all Newbie's."

George, "He was with the 571st Medical Detachment, Phu Bai." (On loan)

Dave, "That's me on the right, at that point I was kind of a new AC, I think I was in country maybe 6 months at that time."

Voice from audience, "Yeah, you look real old there." (Laughter.)

Dave, "Anyway, they kinda sent us off into the wild there. There's Eddie Iacobacci, Ed was a great Medic and a good guy. Eddie Hopper, he was the Crew Chief, he really took care of this thing, he polished it, he was responsible for this bright yellow thing, this Curious Yellow thing, he was a wild and crazy guy that did that. We used to be able to get away with stuff like that. Nobody knew quite what it meant or what it was about, or whether it was illicit or against the rules or whatever but Eddie did it. Eddie liked weapons. He had different machine guns and he had grenade launchers and he had all kinds of stuff he carried with him."

Eddie Hopper, Crew Chief

Medic Ed Iacobacci

George Shaughnessy

"There's George. I tell you what, he blew my mind; here we are, going out with some trepidation to the helicopter, we knew it was going to be messy. There's Shaughnessy. He announced to Hopper that he was going. It was a command decision on his part, he was part of the crew and that was it. Oh, OK, we didn't have any say about it. It was great. Thank You!"

"I'm not positive if this was taken in route on this mission, but it's possible that might have been the final flight." (Hopper later said this photo was taken before the final flight.) "Anyway, here's a photo of Curious Yellow in the air with background typical to that situation."

**Khe Sanh runway in middle distance, Hill 950.
Note helicopter on the pad.**

"When we got out there, the situation was kind of "all's quiet on the western front" except around Hill 950 where it wasn't quiet. It was quiet because there were no ARVNs or Americans, it was all NVA and they had control of the whole thing. They decided that Firebase Hickory, as it was known, was over; it was a thorn in their side long enough. This wasn't just a spontaneous attack, it was a well planned attack and we have documents to go along with that."

"Here is Roger Hill about an hour or so before we picked him up. He got injured at various times during that morning but one of the things that happened was when he got up, the Bru strikers came in."

Roger, "The Bru montagnards came in and said, 'VC number 10,' that's all they could say. They kept pointing down towards the valley and I was looking over the foot trench, over sandbags, and I'm looking down in the valley and I couldn't see anything.

I'm looking and looking and couldn't see anything and finally... We had concertina wire and c-ration cans we'd throw out there... Finally I laid my eyes on a 20-pound Chicom Claymore that was staring me right in the face out there in the weeds. The Bru was pointing to the clay-more. Sappers had come up in the nighttime and after going around the perimeter, had set up 7 of them in key positions. They were there to knock down helicopters. They were like giant shotgun shells, they were set up in positions where a helicopter would come in."

Dave, "Roger went out there and that's where he got his first injury, someone shot a rocket at him, an RPG, and he got various shrapnel wounds and so forth, then he came back in. He had to keep carrying on because they were under attack now. The guy who's standing there with his head kinda clipped off is John Caviani. This is about the best picture we have of him. He was the last American there. He earned the Congressional Medal of Honor for his actions that day. Because he stayed and put down suppressive fire so the helicopters could come in and get the people out.

They were in serious trouble. They were surrounded.

And you guys who flew Dustoff will recognize this part of the story. They didn't happen to mention that they had already broken into the wire." "Yeah, we're in a firefight and we've got some injuries and come on down" and they didn't happen to mention that the enemy was already inside the compound! I didn't know this until years later after talking to Roger!"

"We flew in just below the level of the pinnacle, there was no way to just fly in from above or we would just get shot out of the air with no question, so we flew up the side of the mountain to the wall right at the end. I just pulled cyclic back and popped it up and flared up to set it down. When we got a better angle, I'm looking out where it's all crazy and I couldn't find a place to land.

I'm just hovering there, looking around and precious seconds are going by. We finally found some place to set down and luckily it was near where Roger was. It was a miracle, it wasn't calculated at all. Things were way too chaotic at that point. Roger got thrown in, we were only there for a few seconds, maybe 5 seconds at most, we weren't there for a long time at all.

As soon as we set it down, there were explosions all around. This was as scared as I've ever been, I really hadn't been in anything like this before. Stuff was exploding right in front of the windshield. I always thought it was mortars, I didn't understand the situation then. Roger told me later, 'Nah, those weren't mortars, they were throwing hand grenades at you!' That's great!

We just dumped it off the side and we used to do this thing that Steve Woods and Joel Dozhier kinda called, "The Falling Leaf." It was a really wonderful erratic thing that had to be very controlled, stay in trim and all that stuff. We turned sideways and it's just like a pickup truck falling off the side of a cliff, only all the emergency lights came on and the hydraulics went out and all of a sudden the controls weren't working right and the fuel is going down.

During the flight out, we just had enough fuel to get back to Quang Tri and I could see that wasn't looking right. It really was looking pretty bad there for a couple seconds.

The Air Force had an F4 that been shot up in the area and had to go back to Da Nang, so they had some aircraft there and I remember they had a controller up above and he's yellin', 'Dustoff's down! Dustoff's down!' And we've got all the radios going and I'm squeezing the radio button, 'No were not, God Damn it! No, we're not goin' down.' We're going all sideways, falling to the ground and Iacobacci is back there yellin', 'Stay Cool, stay cool for Christ's sake! Fly the aircraft!' I shot back, 'I am cool!' It was the most, un-cool possible scene ever imagined. But somehow, the thing leveled out, with me and Kreger pulling on the controls, it leveled out.

Steve Woods and Joel Dozhier, bless those guys, Steve was second up and he brought a ship out there. He was kind of my mentor and he wanted to oversee, 'his student.' And Joel Dozhier, it was his last day in country, he was leaving the next day to go to Saigon, but he stole a helicopter, he just went out there and they're out there flying around.

We're goin' down and there's Woods calling us on the radio, 'Well, you got white smoke comin' out of the back and...' So we do this running landing on the airstrip, that old PCP airstrip at Khe Sanh, it wasn't in too good of shape. That's what Roger's complaining about, he claims we bounced his head.

Somehow we got the thing down and came to a stop, these two guys (Woods and Dozhier) were right there behind us. We would have been taken prisoners for sure. Shaughnessy jumps out with his .60 machine gun, he runs out like an infantry guy and he sets up his perimeter; Hopper sets up his perimeter, and the guys from the other ship are running over to get the patients, Roger and a couple of the Brus. They threw them all in the other aircraft. Shaughnessy was the last one to get on the other helicopter; he kinda closed out his perimeter. We took off over the top of Curious Yellow, and I remember the blades were still turning. Then I noticed the rotating beacon was still on and I thought, 'Ah, shit, I forgot to turn off the rotating beacon. What a shitty pilot!'

The helicopter was retrieved weeks later. The situation wasn't conducive to other helicopters showing up. It has a lot of bullet holes in it, but I think a bunch of those bullet holes were from Cobra pilots shooting it up later for fun. I'm not positive about that. But we did sustain a lot of bullet holes.

When we got back I expected our commander to tell me what a great deal it was and all that and basically what he said was, "You left with a helicopter!"

Still speaking to the group in attendance, Dave had this to say:

"It's an interesting story to meet up, and every one of you have done stuff like this and every one of you has picked someone up in this kind of situation. It's a blessing and a rare honor to actually meet someone that you picked up, so I have to thank everyone who made that possible."

Warrant Officer Steve Wood, Aircraft Commander of the covering Dustoff helicopter, had this to add,

"The courage and dedication of the Special Forces (SF) teams and troops that maintained the high ground surrounding the former Marine base at Khe Sanh was truly legendary. All of us who had lived and operated out of the airfield at Khe Sanh during Lam Son 719 knew that without these SF teams we would have been unable to keep Khe Sanh open. As you can imagine, taking and holding those hilltops was not without cost. Requests for Medevac, was all too common from all of these outposts with Hill 950 being one of the most frequent. Most of the crews who had flown Dustoff out of Khe Sanh during Lam Son 719 had been into Hill 950 at least once. Some of us, including Dustoff 702 had been in several times.

It was definitely not a place you wanted to make a pick up from unless there was no option available.

On the day Dustoff 702 "Curious Yellow" was shot down, we had been pretty busy. We had 2 ships flying what was called "First-Up" in the area West of Quang Tri. I had just finished refueling when a request came into DMZ Dustoff to evacuate approximately 12–20 WIA's from Hill 950. Dave Hansen (Dustoff 702) and I (Dustoff 509) both responded to the request. After arriving on scene we set up an orbit over the valley Southwest of Khe Sanh to make up a game plan and coordinate with the guys on the ground. The sitrep (tactical situation report) was not good news. The SF team in control of Hill 950 advised us that they had been fighting the NVA "inside the wire" and were receiving mortar, RPG, .51cal and small arms fire. They further stated that only one end of the base was suitable for landing because the "friendly's" at the other end of the base were still in a firefight and recommended that we approach from the west and depart in the same direction. We were further advised to wait for a few minutes until the WIA's were re-positioned for evacuation.

As the sitrep was being radioed to us, you could hear automatic weapons fire and explosions in the background and see the gray and black smoke from rounds hitting the base.

After orbiting for several minutes, we decided that because Dave Hansen (Dustoff 702) was lower on fuel than we were, they would make the first pick-up. I advised the RTO on Hill 950 that we (the second Dustoff) would be on the ground as soon as the first Dustoff cleared the LZ and to keep the remaining WIA's in the LZ and be ready for immediate loading. After working things out, Dave started his approach to Hill 950. It was a textbook tactical approach to a hilltop where troops were in contact. Everything looked good as Dave popped his aircraft up over the berm on the cliff side of the LZ and came to a low hover over the bunkers. From my vantage point, (having already started my approach to the LZ) it appeared that Dave was being directed to move around in the LZ and where to land and make the pick-up. Not something you normally wanted to do, but, under the circumstances with the very limited space where a landing would be advisable, you had to pay attention to the guys on the ground and land exactly where they wanted you.

Dave and his crew had been on the ground for less than 15 or 20 seconds when mortars, RPG's and/or grenades started exploding right in front of and next to their aircraft. We could only watch while they held their position and continue loading patients while coming under an intense barrage of enemy fire. Clearly the NVA had the LZ zeroed in and had been waiting for a helicopter to arrive. As soon as the crew of Dustoff 702 finished loading patients, someone (from Dustoff 702) radioed that they were "coming out". Even as they were departing the LZ, you could see their aircraft continue to take hits. They had barely become airborne when copious amounts of white smoke and what appeared to be fuel began pouring out of their helicopter. From our vantage point it looked like they were going down on the mountainside just below the SF Base where much of the NVA fire was coming from. It was both a miracle and extraordinary piloting skills that kept "Curious Yellow" from crashing in the jungle where survival would have been all but impossible.

As Dave and his crew were getting "Curious Yellow" under control, we broke off our approach to Hill 950 and joined up on them in a loose formation.

Dave advised me that their hydraulics were gone and that they were losing fuel. He further advised that they were going to attempt an emergency (hydraulics off) landing on the abandoned airstrip at Khe Sanh. While still trailing smoke and fluids, Dave and his crew did a masterful job of making a run-on landing at Khe Sanh without catching fire or crashing the heavily laden and severely damaged helicopter. After landing our aircraft next to "Curious Yellow" the patients were transferred to our helicopter by both of our crews. While the transfer was taking place, it was comforting to see Sgt. Shaughnessy with his M-60 and one of the crew from Dustoff 702 with his Thompson providing security. As soon as the patients were loaded, the crew of Dustoff 702 boarded our helicopter and we flew to the 18th Surgical Hospital in Quang Tri.

The dedication to the mission and courage under fire as demonstrated by the crew of Dustoff 702 on Hill 950 was what Dustoff was all about. Dave and the crew of "Curious Yellow" were my friends. Long before that June day in 1971, all of them had earned my friendship and respect. The mission to evacuate the WIA's from Hill 950 is another example of what these guys (and all the Dustoff crews) did day after day.

Most of the time we never knew what happened to "our" patients, but every once in a while, a story like this one comes back to life, and our memories are rekindled. This mission was one that none of the people involved will ever forget. It's good to hear that life has gone on and been good for those that survived that day on Hill 950. All the best, Steve Woods, Dustoff 509.

Warrant Officer Steve Woods

Mission 14

Young & Stupid

This is a story that first appeared in the magazine *VIETNAM* in the April 2004 issue. It is reprinted here with a few changes. Phil Marshall.

In Order To Be Old And Wise
One Must First Be Young And Stupid
Ancient U.S. Army Proverb

I arrived in Vietnam on the 4th of July 1969, barely 21 years old. It was an average age for most of the other Army helicopter pilots I flew with in the 237th Medical Detachment in northern I Corps near the DMZ. One guy was 19, while the oldest (not counting our Commanding Officer) was the 28-year-old XO, Army slang for the second in command Executive Officer. Back home in the real world, my buddies were at the drive-in, drinking beer and looking for a carload of girls to flirt with, just as I had been doing a year or two before. Even though I had yet to fly my first hour of combat, I had already done many incredible things that my high school and college friends could not even dream of.

I couldn't have been more proud of my flight school classmates and myself for having come this far. With a fair amount of apprehension, it was now "the moment of truth." Could we really do what we had been trained to do without letting anyone down? We especially were concerned about the troops we were there to support. It was finally time to find out if we had the "gonads" to be combat helicopter pilots.

When I found out that I was assigned to be a Medevac pilot, I was devastated. In my mind, the only way I would survive the 365 days in Southeast Asia was to be a gunship pilot, blazing my way back to the states, defending myself with mini-guns, rockets and grenade launchers. All through flight school, we were taught by gun pilots, slick drivers, scout pilots (although not as many of the scout pilots, they had a high loss ratio) and oh, yes, ONE Dustoff pilot. He was an instructor pilot at Downing Army Airfield at Ft. Wolters, Texas in May of 1968. I remember my very first primary flight instructor pointing at him as I listened intently to his every word. "There walks a dead man. He was a Dustoff pilot."

"A dead man" meaning he should never have made it back since Dustoff aircraft were unarmed Medevac helicopters with red and white targets painted all over them and flew single ship missions. It was a fact that Dustoff crews had 3 times the casualty rate of other helicopter crews. I never forgot the reverence with which that statement was made, as I began to form a "survival plan of action" in my mind. I would NOT fly unarmed helicopters!

Shortly after arriving at Ft. Rucker, Alabama, I learned that those of us with the highest flight grades would attend a two-week gun school near the end of training while the rest learned formation flying. I wanted that top 20% and focused all my abilities and energy on making gunship training. I did well enough to make the school along with about 25 of my classmates. But as the Army would have it, during Friday night formation of the middle weekend of gun school, 24 of us, including 12 in the gun school, received orders to attend Medevac school at Ft. Sam Houston, Texas, immediately after graduation. I told my roommate, "This is it. I won't make it back." Obviously, I was wrong but I didn't know it then.

It turned out to be the best thing that happened to me, even though I was wounded before the year was out and sent home before my tour was over.

I had no idea of the satisfaction, pride, sense of accomplishment and even elation that I would feel in the next six months.

Since I first heard the phrase that is the title of this article, it struck me that those words were exactly what we did as "kids" flying helicopters in Vietnam. As I look back on my own experiences, two things stand out in my mind that I consider "young and stupid." First of all, there was landing on the Navy Hospital ships USS Repose and USS Sanctuary in the South China Sea very near the Demilitarized Zone. While in themselves, those landings were not stupid, the way we got there was! Our single engine UH-1H Hueys did not float in the water very well. In fact, not at all since we usually flew with the doors open, even at night. And what was even "stupider" I suppose was the fact that if the doors were closed when we reached the water, we opened them so we could get out easier if we did go down. Okay, so the Hueys were extremely reliable, and I still love those incredible machines, but for the moment let us discuss navigation equipment on a Huey.

And the answer is: "There IS none!" Sure, we had a compass and an Automatic Direction Finder, but in the event of an engine failure on the way to the hospital ship, this would have probably been my emergency call.

"Mayday, Mayday, Mayday, Dustoff 7-1-1, we're going down over the sea. We're about 5 miles out." Five miles out from where? Maybe it was only 3 miles... No, 7! Shoot, I had NO idea! But come look for us, will ya? We'll try to leave an oil slick or something!

But I suppose we would have survived; we had water wings! Mine were draped over the back of my seat, along with my M-16 rifle. It was a well known (and very true) fact that during an emergency exit from an aircraft, if you don't have it strapped to your body, you won't take it with you. If I had gone down over land, I probably wouldn't have taken my weapon with me. If I had gone down over water, I wouldn't have grabbed the "wings" either, because not only had I never tried to inflate them, I had never even tried to put them on. Well, maybe we could have used our survival radio once we were in the water or forced down over the jungle. Hehehehe... Survival radio, what's that? Is that AM or FM? Can I pick up Armed Forces Radio on it? We HAD no survival radios in those aircraft.

(So I guess that makes three "Young and Stupids.")

Once out to sea, landing on the ships was an interesting experience in itself, especially when the decks were bouncing up and down like a fishing bobber with a carp under it.

I already knew the difference between port and starboard and it wasn't that hard to figure out "beam" and "quartering" approaches. I used to laugh at the occasional Huey slick driver who flew out to let guys from his unit use the shopping facilities on the ships. The radioman on the ship would tell them "Cleared for a port quarter approach." The silence on the radio was the proverbial "pregnant pause" and I could imagine the conversation inside the Huey cockpit. "What'd he say?" "Hell, I don't know. Damn Navy talk!" The hospital ship would then radio to the helicopter again "Just come in from the left and land to the back of the boat." It always got an immediate "Roger!"

It has been said many times by Navy and Marine jet pilots that landing on an aircraft carrier is like landing on a postage stamp.

I would never dispute that, but I would argue that putting a helicopter on the tiny pad of the hospital ship is like landing on a corner of that postage stamp. And nighttime was even worse. The first time I tried to land on the ship at night, I terminated at a 30-foot hover over the deck instead of on the deck and the Aircraft Commander had to take over and hover us down to the ship. That was probably the lowest point of my Vietnam flying experience, and I never forgot it.

I promised myself that it would never happen again and it didn't. It wasn't easy and I will now confess that my depth perception almost was not good enough to pass my initial flight physical, but I made it. (As an aside, when I returned to the states later and applied for my military drivers license so I could drive the Company pick-up truck, I was told I didn't pass the depth perception portion of the eye test and would not be issued the license. I was OK to fly helicopters in the Army, but not to drive a jeep! I asked to take a different test and was able to pass that one!) Knowing that my depth perception left little margin for error on the night approaches (especially), I had to totally concentrate on what I was doing and not relax for a second until we were down on that rockin' and rollin' ship.

The night I was wounded, my new Co-Pilot Don Study put us right on the deck, but all the while I had visions of my first 30-foot hover when I was a Funny New Guy - an FNG. I knew that if Don got in trouble on the approach, I could not be of much help because of the gunshot wound in my left arm, but we were Young and Stupid and we made it. I will always thank Warrant Officer Study for his late night "picture perfect" landing on the round end of the boat.

Oh, were we Young and Stupid on hoist missions, too; the second Y & S thing we did! As Medevac helicopter pilots, we flew the only Army Hueys equipped with the electric hoist/winch. The most incredible, dangerous, high pucker-factor, exhilarating thing a man can do with a helicopter is to pull an unsecured hoist mission, day or night. Add to that, it is also the most unforgiving mission flown in a helicopter. First, one has to understand what a hoist mission is and why we did them. Generally, someone is badly wounded in jungle or mountainous (or both) terrain where a helicopter cannot land on the ground or even close to it. The tactical situation is such that the ground troops cannot get the dead or wounded to a secure open area for evacuation.

We must now hover over the trees or rocky terrain while we let out up to 150-feet of quarter inch cable with a Madaffer Jungle Penetrator or a Stokes Litter attached to it. Translation: There's bad guys all around, we've got wounded, get in here NOW before they die or we have more wounded and you have to come back again.   We don't have anyplace for you to land, so just hang your butts out in the open sky for several minutes so any kid with a bow and arrow can shoot you down and Gee, those red crosses on your helicopter sure make great aiming points, don't they?   When you crash, we'll try to recover your bodies.

We were unarmed and experience taught us that usually, we were better off to quickly fly to the landing zone, get in and get out as fast as possible while avoiding the bad guys and fly straight back to the hospital.   If we waited for gunship support, it may be too late for the wounded, so most times we tried to "sneak in" and "sneak out" (if that's possible in a clattering helicopter) and complete the rescue before the enemy had TOO much time to shoot us up... Or down.

A hoist mission was just the opposite. We still got there in a hurry, but once there, we hovered over the trees like a target at the county fair 25-cent shooting booth.

Five minutes or more seemed like hours while we sat in the air over the ground troops, taxing every bit of professionalism that we had. And the reader better believe we had the utmost professionalism. The crewmen I flew with on hoist missions (like me, in their teens and early 20's) were absolutely the best and I wish I could shake every one of their hands and hug them today. I am so very proud to have served with them. It required every skill we had. If we had been shot down on virtually any hoist mission, our high hover would not have allowed us to make a safe landing and many would surely die. That was the unforgiving part.

It happened many times, and their names are on the Wall in Washington, D.C.

One particular mission I recall was a day hoist. We were an easier target during the day, but unlike at night when we kept all the lights off, we could see what we were doing! When we were on short final approach over the landing zone, I heard small arms fire and my "brand new" Crew Chief yelled, "We're taking fire!" I pulled power into the rotor system to get out of there as quickly as I could when the radio operator on the ground called out "Dustoff, where are you going?" "We're taking fire," I said.

"That was us giving you covering fire!" he replied. "OK, I'm turning around" and I did another Young & Stupid thing; I made a pedal turn (U-turn) about 200 feet in the air, probably over some bad guys, and hovered back in over the trees.

Normally, one has to push a button to talk over the intercom in a military aircraft, but on a hoist mission, we turned it to "hot mikes" because we all needed our hands for other things. With a "hot mike" everything that was said, every noise, every round fired, every grunt and groan was amplified and transmitted into everyone's headset without touching any buttons.

A constant line of chatter was transmitted from the Medic and the Crew Chief to the pilots, who were both on the flight controls in case either was violently incapable of continuing to fly the aircraft. (One has to realize that there was virtually no protection for the pilots from the front and little from the sides or underneath.)

"The cable's going out... About halfway down... Come right... It's on the ground...

Looking good... Come forward just a little... Keep your tail straight... Come left... They're on the penetrator..." was typical of the continual commentary from the enlisted crewmembers.

As the Aircraft Commander in control of the helicopter, my eyes never left the tree branches that were touching the nose of my aircraft, but made flight adjustments according to the guys in the back. The additional weight of patients on the end of the hoist as they were lifted off the ground further complicated the stability of the aircraft. During a hoist mission, we flew with one finger on a button on the cyclic stick that operated a cable-cutting device. The pilot could instantly sever the cable should any part of the lift apparatus get snagged in the trees or in any other emergency situation. Otherwise, if we got tangled up, it could cause the aircraft to crash. I wonder how many grunts would have gotten on the hoist had they known about that button.

When I read the quickly handwritten sheet for this particular mission, I knew before we left that it was going to be an unsecured hoist, so we grabbed some unsuspecting "schmuck," told him to get his weapon and some ammo and run with us to the aircraft.

We put him in the back of the cargo compartment with his M-16 and a helmet, hooked him up to the intercom and we were off. I have no idea who he was, but we logged his flight time as "PP - Patient Protector."

After the first of the two injured soldiers were hoisted on board, the din of the covering fire began to register in my head. With the front of my Huey still kissing the tree leaves and my crew keeping me posted as to what was going on, I took a quick, curious look out my left window to see where the friendly fire was impacting. "Oh, Sugar!" (Not my exact word.) "I can throw a rock in there, it's so close!" was the rest of my thought. I then realized that ole PP back there was just sitting in the hell- hole taking it all in, not doing a thing! "Put some fire in that bunker!" I yelled to Private What's-His-Name. I guess that woke him up, as the next thing I heard was his rifle plugging away at a mound of dirt just outside his door and about 30 feet down.

The rest of the mission went as expected with no more surprises. We took no hits on that mission and as we lifted out of the landing zone, the fact that we "cheated death" again left me with all the exciting feelings I mentioned at the beginning of this article.

There was an adrenaline high, too, and a tremendous sense of accomplishment that I have yet to experience since flying my last mission in Vietnam. The emotions are almost indescribable, but there was one more feeling. Relief from being so scared!

Being scared in the sense of risking one's life for others, for sure, but also a sense of being scared that you won't be up to the standards of your fellow pilots. Scared that maybe, just maybe, you'll fail your mission where someone else just like you would have succeeded. I suppose that's what kept most of us going in the daily risk of flying helicopters in combat in Vietnam. If we didn't do it, the next guy would and we would have been found to be personally lacking what it took to complete the mission.

In retrospect, I think that's what happened to one of the pilots in our unit a few months after I left. Warrant Officer 1 Al Gaidis was a tall, curly haired kid as I remember him. Always smiling and never hurt anyone, I would guess.

On what turned out to be his final mission, they were to pick up wounded on a mountaintop, but got caught in heavy fire while making their approach.

Whether they took hits at this time or not is speculation, but he tried another tactic. He dropped to the deck a couple miles out and then screamed up the hill at 120 knots and treetop level, trying to "sneak in" past the enemy.

But this time he definitely took hits in a .50 caliber crossfire and as he peeled off from the mountain, fuel was streaming from the aircraft. The gunships that were escorting him told Al to put it on the ground right away because of the serious leak. "I think I can make it to the river!" was the last message as the aircraft caught fire, rolled inverted and crashed in flames, killing all on board. My opinion is that he was as afraid that he couldn't complete the mission as much as he was afraid to die. At least, I believe that's how I would have felt had it been me. We always at least tried to complete the mission and felt that we let someone down if we didn't. We risked much on these missions but there was no doubt that we were very appreciated!

So, were we really Young and Stupid? Yes, most definitely young, but stupid? I don't think so.

We all volunteered to do something that only a year or two before we could not have even dreamed that we would be doing. Something that only a very few could ever experience; something for which only a very few could even qualify.

Those of us lucky enough to come home learned from the excursion, and were without question, changed men and no longer wide-eyed boys.

I think that some of us changed for the better, but some of us didn't. I tried to use the opportunity to prove to myself that I could accomplish the goals that I set for myself and do them well. In fact, we all did well. As a group, we helicopter pilots and our crews did what we had to do and then some. We sacrificed our youth and innocence; we achieved above and beyond the call of duty on a daily basis. Not only were we not found to be lacking as youthful aviators, as a whole we far exceeded the expectations. We are now Older and Wiser, and for that I am very thankful.

Epilogue:

Most people who see photos of Dustoff Hueys in Vietnam observe only the outside of the aircraft.

Only a few privileged people other than the crewmembers themselves know an obscure fact that there were actually 3 seats in the cockpit of a Dustoff helicopter rather than two seats as mounted in other Hueys. The third seat was for our testicles.

Although I was sworn to secrecy at the time, with the Freedom of Information Act I believe that I can now break that silence.

When we, as students, first began training in Hueys at Ft. Rucker, Alabama, our Instructor Pilots (IPs) were required to fill out a Department of the Army (DA) form if our testicles were too big to fit comfortably in the standard front seat of a Huey. This form number DA-4733-DSC (Dustoff Sized Cajones), was used to determine which pilots would obtain Medevac training at Ft. Sam Houston, Texas, upon completion of training at Mother Rucker. The DA-4733-DSC should not be confused with the much more common DA-4734-GSTT (Gunship Sized Tiny Testicles). The third seat was installed in our combat aircraft to accommodate the well above average size of our family jewels; which were required to complete most of the missions that we flew in Vietnam.

Of course, the Crew Chiefs and Medics in the back had super-sized balls; too, but they had the whole cargo compartment for theirs!

Have you ever heard the expression, "He was flying the aircraft balls out?" That was us. Dustoff pilots and their unique seating arrangement is where that statement originated.

On the ground, the troops would look up at Hueys flying over. When they saw one flying "balls out" they knew it was a Dustoff on an urgent mission. There was a down side to the oversized appendages, however. As mentioned earlier, there was little protection from weapon fire for the pilots and with body parts exposed on a third seat, we were especially vulnerable. One pilot lost a testicle to a .50 caliber round and was only able to father 44 children (at last count) after returning from overseas. (Personally, I have fathered 73 children with two good Dustoff sized testicles.) We know that it was a .50 cal that got him and not an AK47 bullet because an AK round is not big enough to shoot off the balls of a Dustoff pilot. But it was a small price to pay for the successful completion of our daily rescues.

Further proof of these facts can be found at a recent Vietnam Helicopter Pilots Association (VHPA) reunion.

As an elevator at the reunion hotel was transporting myself and other attendees to the Saturday night banquet, another Dustoff pilot stepped on from his floor. As he entered the crowded car, his only comment was "Ball room, please."

The others on board simply assumed that he was also headed for dinner, but I knew the true meaning of his statement. I just tapped him gently on the shoulder and whispered, "Hey, Buddy, I'm as far back in the elevator as I can get now." I knew what he really was saying.

In closing, I would merely like to state that I am able to write this today in large part because of luck. A whole lot of GOOD luck and a little bit of good humor."

Mission 15

LOSS OF JOE BROWN
AND
THE ORDEAL OF DENNIS FUJII

Author's note: As discussed elsewhere in this book, Lam Son 719 was ill-conceived and a giant fiasco in my opinion. On paper, it probably looked great, but in reality, many, many good helicopter crewmen died, or were wounded, and many, many perfectly good helicopters were lost. Many feel the men and aircraft were lost needlessly. Most of us who supported the ARVNs, Army of the Republic of South Vietnam, the good guys, seem to agree that for the most part, the ARVNs did not want to fight but it was certainly OK if the Americans did the dirty work for them. Time after time, especially during 719, perfectly able ARVN soldiers would abandon their positions, jumping on helicopters, sometimes swarming them, if the battle was particularly nasty. Pilots in the 237th could not land sometimes because too many would try to climb aboard, so a high hover was held while the wounded were loaded while keeping the healthy soldiers from climbing in the aircraft. Even then, they would grab onto the skids in an attempt to leave the battle.

Crews then began greasing the skids so they could not hold on. With the weight of extra bodies hanging on, there were times that the helicopters could not fly.

It was during my next to last day flying in Vietnam that we received a night time mission to pick up one or two wounded South Vietnamese soldiers. We were inundated by onrushing soldiers and I had to take off before I knew whether we had the wounded or not. We were simply filled to the gills and we couldn't take any more! Shortly after taking off, I called the guys in the back, "How many do we have?" After several seconds, one of the guys called back, "Looks like about 15, Sir!" Even if we did have the wounded on board, there was no way the Medic would have even been able to get to them. We had 19 souls on board that night; we just took them to the hospital and dumped them off. Let their Commanders sort out the wounded and those who just wanted out of the battle!

Medic Paul Simcoe writes: I guess I have my own story to relate, it was probably the worst day I had in Vietnam, and the closest I came to "grabbing my ankles." This was the mission I was on with Dennis Fujii.

This was Feb. 18th, 1971; we were called to a hill in Laos, about 15 klicks from Khe Sanh, I guess; there was a company of ARVN rangers there, who called us to pick up some wounded. We asked if there had been any contact, they said no, no contact for two days. As we approached the hill, we realized they had not been quite forthcoming with us, they were taking fire from every direction, including artillery and mortars, the whole hill was covered in smoke. This place, it turns out, was surrounded by about a division of NVA, deeply entrenched. We tried several approaches, and took fire every time, though we were coming in low level. We finally, I think on the third try, came in from the south, and just as we were about to land, some ARVNs who had been holding up wounded, dropped their wounded and ran for the chopper. The NVA started "walking" mortars, and the third or fourth one got us right under the nose of the aircraft; this was followed by a monsoon of every kind of weapon they had. Somehow the pilots managed to land the craft, even though at that time they had both already been hit by that first mortar, though I didn't know it yet. Joe Brown, first pilot, was hit in the chest, and Monteith, Co-Pilot, who had only been in country 2 weeks, was hit at the base of the spine.

The chopper bounced around, steadied itself, and we all jumped out while they were firing small arms, mortars and .50 cal at us; the chopper was a complete Swiss cheese by the time we got out. Fujii and myself crawled into a small ditch (this was formerly an NVA base, so the ditches were very narrow, they being quite small people, as you recall; we barely fit in them). Fujii told me he was hit. I was the Medic, so I crawled over him in the ditch (we were facing each other), and took care of his shoulder wound, which wasn't bad. The whole time they were firing an incredible amount of mortars and small arms at us, plus a relentless .50 cal. Among the ARVN that had called us, many were wounded or dead. I don't know how many there were, I think about a company. They were not in any fighting condition any more, they were just holed up in tiny bunkers scattered on the hill.

I asked one of the ARVNs to take me to a radio, he didn't want to because there was just too much fire going on, and we had to crawl above ground to get to it. I was desperate, so I grabbed him and forced him to take me to the radio, which ended up being in the bunker where my two pilots were. Joe Brown was in pretty bad shape already.

I got on the radio and actually got hold of somebody, told them our position, and what had happened. After I don't know how long, maybe an hour, we heard a chopper coming in, so myself, and two very wobbly pilots got out of the bunker and made our way toward the arriving chopper.

As the chopper arrived, it was maybe 20 feet from us, it took a withering amount of fire, and I saw the pilot's desperate face, eyes like saucers, shaking his head at me, meaning he couldn't make the landing. One or two people on his chopper got hit during this attempt, from what I heard later. So we were left out there in the open, chopper flying away, and of course Charlie redoubled his efforts to erase us with much gusto. We hit the dirt, a mortar hit very close to us, I got hit (back, arm and butt), and Joe Brown got hit again, in the chest again, much worse than me. Monteith and I crawled to a nearby bunker, he couldn't walk any more because of his spine injury, but we were basically crawling anyway. Joe was moaning right outside the bunker, asking for water, but there was just too much fire for me to go out and drag him in. I tried, believe me, but there was almost continuous automatic weapons fire right outside the entrance of the bunker.

Every time I made an attempt, I was met with a wall of bullets. They knew we were there, and they were real close.

I had found a homing beacon of some sort, so I turned it on and placed it right at the bunker entrance. There was another attempt to rescue us from our unit, but that chopper took too much fire also, so it flew away. At this point Monteith couldn't feel his legs anymore, I was bleeding a fair amount, and Joe was just a few feet away, unreachable, and moaning. Monteith took his .38 out, looked at it, and I wondered what was going through his mind. I asked him; he just said, "Well..." I knew I didn't want to be captured alive by these guys, and that may have been on his mind too. Maybe we could take a couple of them before they finished us. It sounded like Charlie was coming closer now, up the hill, the small arms sounded real close, and no one left to fight back. After some time, we suddenly heard all hell break loose, it turned out to be some Cobras that basically made a perimeter of fire around us, blazing everything they had, automatic grenade launchers, rockets, mini-guns, all at the same time, and a slick landed in the middle of the circle, door gunners firing the whole time.

At this point, my junior Medic Costello came out from somewhere, found Joe and dragged him to the slick, while I half-carried, half dragged Monteith to it.

SP4 COSTELLO

Somehow we made it to the chopper, and it took off. I guess we made it out thanks to the Cobras, and somebody told me later that some F-4's had dropped napalm over an enemy position north of us, just prior to this attempt. I realized immediately that we were missing somebody, namely Fujii. No one had seen him, so we didn't know if he was still alive. He ended up coming back five days later, after some pretty harrowing experiences, but that is his story.

Joe was sinking fast as we made our way back to Khe Sanh. One thing I will never get out of my mind, or my heart, is when he grabbed my hand, held it tight, and said, "Don't let me die, Simcoe."

I was sure he would make it, we were only minutes away, and we had made it through this hell. So I told him I was sure he would make it. But his hand all of a sudden slackened its grip completely, his eyes closed, and his breathing became much more labored. We arrived at Khe Sanh, I told the Medic to take Brown out first, there was an aid station there. I asked the doc there if Joe would make it, and he sadly shook his head, "no." I couldn't believe it. They put Joe on the stretcher there in the aid tent, and he just suddenly sat up, said, "I can't breathe!" and fell back dead. That was basically one minute after arriving at Khe Sanh.

Medic Paul Simcoe at his post inside the aircraft, behind the right pilot's seat. The helmet he is wearing was lost during the mission narrated here.

Monteith eventually made it back, he was shipped to Japan I believe and then to the U.S. and I heard that he is well and walking.

I roamed around for a few years after the army, not doing anything productive, kind of angry and bitter. I had been a high school dropout. But eventually I went to college, and then Medical school, and I have been an ER doc for the past 20 or so years.

Phil, I have to tell you, it was a bit difficult writing this. I hadn't revisited these memories in a very long time.

One thing I would ask, is that if Joe Brown's parents are still around, I don't think it would be nice for them to read how Joe died. We always tell the folks, "He didn't feel it" and that's the way it should be. So if this story is ever published, in whatever form, I would ask that he either make sure that Joe's parents are no longer with us, or if they are, change the name so they are protected from unnecessary suffering. Paul Simcoe

CW2 Joe Brown, Pilot, left, with Pilot 1LT Alan Rhodes, digging their sleeping quarters at Khe Sanh during Lam Son 719.

Author's note: Next, I offer this account of Crew Chief SP5 Dennis M. Fujii and his time on the ground in Laos. Rather than try to rewrite what has already been written several times, this account is taken from the US ARMY MEDICAL DEPARTMENT, OFFICE OF MEDICAL HISTORY website. The address is:

History.Amedd.Army.Mil/BooksDocs/Vietnam/Dustoff/Chapter5.html

Joe Brown was posthumously awarded the Silver Star for Gallantry. His family was good enough to sent a copy of the citation for inclusion here. It reads:

For gallantry in action while engaged in military operations involving conflict with an armed hostile force in the Republic of Vietnam. Chief Warrant Officer W2 Brown distinguished himself while commanding a helicopter ambulance during a rescue operation in the Republic of Laos. Two rescue attempts to retrieve the wounded South Vietnamese were aborted due to the heavy volume of enemy fire.

On the third attempt, Warrant Officer Brown landed and remained on station until all patients were loaded.

Suddenly his helicopter was struck by a barrage of enemy mortar rounds, critically damaging the aircraft and wounding the Commander. After taking cover in a nearby bunker, Mr. Brown, realizing the urgency for Medical evacuation helicopters, raced to the wreckage amid intense enemy mortar and automatic weapons fire in an effort to radio for assistance. During his attempt to call for help, Mr. Brown received additional wounds. Although immediately evacuated to Khe Sanh's Medical facility, he expired upon arrival. Chief Warrant Officer W-2 Brown's gallantry in action, at the cost of his life, was in keeping with the highest traditions of the military service and reflect great credit upon himself, his unit and the United States Army.

"Papa Whiskey"

SPECIALIST 5 DENNIS M. FUJII

One Dustoff mission during the Laos operation illustrated both its chaotic finale and the bravery of a Dustoff crewman.

On 18 February a North Vietnamese regiment assaulted fire support base Ranger North, nine kilometers inside Laos.

About 1130 the South Vietnamese 39th Ranger Battalion holding the base asked the Dustoff operations center at Khe Sanh to evacuate its many seriously wounded. A Dustoff aircraft, with a crew from both the 237th and 571st Detachments, took off and headed west. On their first attempt to land they took such heavy fire that the Commander, CW2 Joseph G. Brown, aborted his approach. A second time around he tried a high speed descent and made it in. Just before the ship touched down the enemy opened fire again and continued firing while the crew loaded the wounded Rangers. Uninjured Rangers trying to escape the base also poured into the ship, and Brown had trouble lifting it off. Just as he cleared the ground, a mortar round exploded in front of the cockpit, shattering the console and wounding him. The ship crashed. Rangers scattered from the wreck and the Dustoff crew dragged Brown to a ditch for temporary shelter. Leaving him with his pilot, CW2 Darrel O. Monteith, the crew chief and two Medical corpsmen started running toward a bunker. A mortar round exploded and blew one corpsman, Sp4c. James C. Costello, to the ground.

His chest protector had saved his life, and he stood up, shaken but uninjured.

The same explosion blew shrapnel into the back and left shoulder of the crew chief, Sp4c. Dennis M. Fujii. A second mortar round wounded the other corpsman, Sp4c. Paul A. Simcoe.

The three men staggered into the bunker. Shortly before 1400 an Eagle Dust-Off ship tried to rescue them, but automatic weapons fire drove it off, wounding its pilot. At 1500 another Eagle Dustoff ship landed under heavy gunship cover. The wounded Dustoff crew, except for Fujii, raced to the Eagle ship. To escape the enemy fire, the Eagle Dustoff pilot had to take off, leaving Fujii as the sole American on the fire base, which was now surrounded by two North Vietnamese regiments. Dennis headed back to the bunker. Another Dustoff ship soon arrived to pick up Fujii, but enemy fire forced it to return to Khe Sanh.

At 1640 Fujii found a working PRC-25 radio and started broadcasting, using the call sign, "Papa Whiskey." He told the pilots high overhead that he wanted no more attempts to rescue him because the base was too hot.

Using what Medical knowledge he had picked up, he began tending to the wounded Rangers who surrounded him.

That night one of the North Vietnamese regiments, supported by heavy artillery, started to attack the small base. For the next seventeen hours "Papa Whiskey" was the nerve center of the allied outpost, using his radio to call in and adjust the fire of U.S. Air Force AC-130 flare ships, AC-119 and AC-130 gunships, and jet fighters. Working with the Air Force's forward air controllers, he coordinated the six flare ships and seven gunships that were supporting Ranger North. Twice during the night the enemy breached the perimeter, and only then did Fujii stop transmitting to pick up an M16 and join the fight.

With the Ranger Commander's per-mission, Fujii brought the friendly fire to within twenty meters of the base's perimeter, often leaving the safety of his bunker to get a closer look at the incoming friendly rounds. He worked all night and into the next mor-ning, bringing in more than twenty coordin-ated gunship assaults.

The next afternoon an all-out rescue attempt began. A fleet of twenty-one helicopters descended on the base, the gunships firing on every possible enemy position. With Fujii also calling in artillery strikes, the allies ringed the camp with continuous fire. Even so hostile fire was so intense that the Commander of the rescue fleet, Lt. Col. William Peachey, prepared to send down a single ship rather than risk a formation. Fujii asked that as many of the 150 ARVN casualties as possible be evacuated before him, but Peachey ordered him to jump on the first ship that landed. Maj. James Lloyd and Capt. David Nelson left the formation, descended into the valley, then flew up a slope to the fire base, hugging the trees, and dropped in unharmed. Fujii scrambled on board with fourteen Rangers. Having recovered from their surprise, the enemy opened fire on the ship as it lifted off. Raked with bullets, it caught fire and the cockpit filled with smoke, The pilots headed toward Ranger South, fire base of the 21st Ranger Battalion about four kilometers southwest. They landed and everyone jumped from the burning ship as its M60 rounds started to cook off in the flames. Miraculously, no one was injured.

Ranger South itself soon came under heavy enemy attack, but Fujii's work was over.

Finally, at 1600 on 22 February, 100 hours after he was wounded, he was admitted to the 85th Evacuation Hospital at Phu Bai. He had helped save 122 Rangers. He was quickly awarded a Silver Star, which was later upgraded to a Distinguished Service Cross.

Fujii's mission was only part of an operation that had turned into an embarrassing scramble to safety. According to the after action report of the 61st Medical Battalion: "During the last phases of Operation Lam Son 719 enemy activity further intensified. Landing zones were dangerously insecure. Air Ambulances landing to pick up wounded were swarmed with fit and able soldiers seeking a way out of their increasingly precarious position. Medical evacuation pilots reported complete lack of discipline during the last days of the operation coupled with extremely hazardous conditions." Evacuation ships, and indeed any aircraft landing near the South Vietnamese units, were rushed by throngs of ablebodied soldiers trying to escape.

One Eagle Dustoff ship, a UH-1H with a normal load of eleven passengers, landed for a pickup and had to take off almost immediately because of small arms fire and mortar rounds in the landing zone.

After the pilot set his ship down in Khe Sanh, his crew counted thirty-two ARVN soldiers on board, all without weapons or equipment, only one of whom was wounded. To prevent ARVN soldiers from hitching a ride back on the sides of the aircraft, some crews resorted to coating the skids with grease.

By early April the Dustoff and Medevac ships had saved hundreds of lives. In the two-month operation they flew some 1,400 missions, evacuating 4,200 patients. Six crewmen were killed and fourteen wounded. Ten air ambulances were destroyed, about one out of every ten aircraft lost in the operation. On 8 April, once the incursion was over, XXIV Corps gave up its operational control of the MEDCOM air ambulances. Dustoff pilots had seen their last major operation of the war.

Dennis Fujii, center facing, Medal of Honor nominee.

I would like to make note to the reader that the story of Dennis Fujii's ordeal has been published more than a few times, including what I have reprinted above from the Army web site. However, during my interviews with him, as you will read, he told me that many of the events he detailed for this work have never been in print before. "No one really asked me the details before until you. They just kinda figured it out from everyone else!" Many of his quotes found here have come to light for the first time ever. Following is his mission as best he can tell it, 40+ years later.

To begin this mission, one of the first things I asked Dennis was how he came up with the call sign, "Papa Whiskey," which are the phonetic alphabet words for the letters "P" and "W." I fully expected something to the effect of, "Well, I figured at the least I would be a Prisoner of War," POW, or something like that. Something with a double meaning. Nope. "That was the call sign that the unit on the ground was using so I just kept using it so everyone would know my location." So much for drama, as if Fujii's experience needed any more drama!

"The crash happened February 18th, and we had a hard landing. The pilots had to jettison the doors to get out and Simcoe and I jumped out of the aircraft. I had received a shrapnel wound that missed my chicken plate. Simcoe helped me take it off and determined that the wound was not serious so he quickly bandaged it. Ranger North was a Base that the NVA had built, so the passages and door-ways were very small. We were in tight quarters at this time, in the trenches.

When the first rescue helicopter landed, someone yelled 'Let's Go!' and we all headed for the aircraft... That's when a barrage of incoming started hitting all around us.

One of the rounds had me zeroed in and when it exploded, I got hit with shrapnel again. This time next to my right eye, and I couldn't see or even stand up. Everything was real blurry for a few seconds, but I could tell the helicopter was taking fire, so I stood up and waved them off. It was obvious the NVA could see the aircraft and they were firing everything they could at it, they took off." Dennis Fujii was now the only American at Ranger North.

"There was no sense losing another helicopter and more men just for me. I remember as they pulled pitch to leave. I know they didn't want to leave me there, I could tell. My immediate thought about my situation was 'Man, you're not gonna make it. Man, you are NOT gonna make it' and I started to get scared. There were about 160 or 170 walking wounded ARVNs on the hill, so I did what I could for them" relying on his "On-The-Job Training" that he received from the 237th and 571st Medics he flew with.

Using a radio that he was able to locate, Dennis began making calls for assistance. One of the first to respond was a light fire team of Cobras, the Dragons of Alpha Battery, 4/77th ARA, Aerial Rocket Artillery.

Dragon Lead was commanded by Jim Fadden with Jack Loadholt serving as Aircraft Commander and Jack's wingman in the second Cobra. There were already fast-movers (jets) in the area, and Jack remembers one of Fujii's first messages, "If you're a fast mover, I need you to hit within 200 meters of me. If you're Cobras, I need you at 50 meters." Loadholt could not get a good view of the LZ from his back seat in the Cobra, but his front seat gunner had a great view and exclaimed "Oh, no, there are bodies flying around down there!"

Even though they were receiving enemy fire and taking hits to the aircraft, the 2 Cobras continued rolling in on their gun runs until their ammo was expended. For their bravery and support of Dennis Fujii, the 2 Aircraft Commanders received Silver Stars and the front seaters received Distinguished Flying Crosses. The pilots were all in agreement, "We didn't know Fujii, but he was one of us, he was our buddy. We were doing everything we could to get him off of that Firebase." At one point of Fujii's ordeal, all the flight crews that were trying to rescue him heard that he had been killed, but things changed the next day when they heard he was still alive and working the radios.

The Americans busted their butts to rescue Dennis Fujii. We continue Dennis' narrative:

"That first night, we lost part of the perimeter. I was able to communicate with many of the ARVN soldiers on the ground and they really were doing their best to survive. The enemy was firing mortars and recoilless rifle rounds… No small arms fire here!

There were 20 or 30 of them coming up the hill behind the barrage and they got into some of the bunkers. The NVA and the ARVNs started throwing hand grenades at each other, they were so close. I guess they were probing our defenses as they left just before dawn. But by morning, we still held the perimeter. I still knew I wasn't gonna make it, but I had to help myself get through it. I just kept waiting."

The next day, the 19th, the enemy continued to fire on the base, but Dennis said that it was much lighter than the day before. Then, about 9:00 in the evening, they started a heavy barrage and it just kept coming. "A C130 'Spooky' gun ship was overhead and was dropping flares, but he couldn't see anything due to the mist in the area that normally forms every evening. I asked him, 'Can't you see the tracers flying around?' and he said he couldn't see anything.

I knew that there was a strobe light in our helicopter, but I would be under fire if I tried to retrieve it. The ARVN base Commander asked me how much fuel was in our aircraft, I told him we had just topped it off before coming out here.

He wanted me to drain the fuel to lessen the chance of an explosion when other rescue aircraft landed under fire. He was afraid that burning fuel might run into the bunker and the fire would be a beacon to the NVA gunners. I was in the Command bunker, near our helicopter, so one of the ARVNs told another soldier to go with me. We headed for the aircraft, and the next thing I know, the guy with me has disappeared... I'm all by myself.

That was when I noticed all these guys running around in the dark. No one was shooting, just running around. I had lost my shirt when Simcoe dressed my wound and I had scrounged up an ARVN shirt which I was now wearing. Apparently no one noticed me as an American, but I think they knew an American was still on the ground and they were looking for me. I got to the bird and found the strobe light but most of the rest of the aircraft had been stripped. I opened a drain valve at the bottom of the aircraft and let it run as I made my way back to the bunker."

Next, Dennis tried to signal the C130 gun ship with the strobe light. "I held it in the air and immediately I started drawing fire!

I thought, 'Holy, Shit' they were so close in the perimeter." But the good guys saw his strobe and advised "Papa Whiskey" they had his position. "I told them, 'Shoot up the whole hill and perimeter! Tell us when so we can take cover!'"

Fujii continues, "I guess the NVA didn't hear Spooky come back because they were caught with their pants down, out in the open. Lots of casualties. We had no re-supply, no ammo, no nothin', I told the ARVNs to take what we had captured and learn to fire the AK-47s.

It was about this time the ARVN Platoon Leader that was with me decided to check on his troops. He left the bunker alone but after a few minutes he came flying back though the entrance and was bleeding from a head wound. I grabbed a small flashlight that they had been using to tune the radio frequencies and saw small streams of blood running down his face. At this point I guess he started to panic as he took out his wallet and started ripping everything up, including his Identification papers. Then he started to rip off his rank and other uniform insignia.

The other ARVNs in the bunker with me all started talking in Vietnamese, pretty much ignoring me. I knew something was up but couldn't figure what was going on. I finally got one of them to tell me the perimeter had been breached. Now I was getting really scared again that we were all going to be killed or captured."

Dennis also knew that the NVA were trying to kick them off the hill, to the point that the ARVNs would try to abandon their position on foot. "They would leave one part of the perimeter untouched, so that one would think that was the best escape route to use since no fire had been received from that direction. But what they would do is set up an ambush down the trail, far enough from the base that you could not go back. You were trapped, so we knew not to try to walk away."

A Cobra pilot had offered to make an attempt to pick him up, but he would have to hang on to the skids or a pylon, something that had been done before as a desperate measure during other exchanges with the enemy. It was a very risky thing to try. "I knew it would not work as everyone would be firing at it when he came in to land.

I told him, 'Thank you, but just keep making gun runs.' I don't remember his call sign, but they were from the 101st Airborne Division."

On the next day, the 20th, a couple of Hueys were able to get in to pick up wounded and resupply, but they were aircraft from another unit, not the 237th or 571st Dustoff units. As he tried to climb on board, the pilot yelled at him to get off and would not let him get on! "Apparently, there was a lot of confusion back at HQ and not everybody knew I was still there or even alive."

Dennis Fujii is a native of Hawaii, and with his oriental appearance and wearing that ARVN shirt, it seems the pilot mistook him for a healthy ARVN and would not let him get on!

"When I was finally picked up, we took a lot of fire coming out of Ranger North and took a lot of hits in the belly, our Huey was badly shot up. We were able to make it to Ranger South, still in Laos, where we crash landed pretty hard. I went head over heels into the back of a pilot's armored seat, injuring my neck and back, leaving a huge knot on my head that is still there today. The Huey started burning, but I was only semi-conscious and still in the aircraft...

One of the ARVNs pulled me out by the arm as the helicopter proceeded to burn to the ground. No explosion, but the ammo was cooking off."

"I found myself sitting in a bunker, a few Hueys were coming in and out but then I realized that I had been left behind again! No more aircraft were coming in! We were taking mortars again, but this time they were less intense. I guess they were just probing us, again, to determine our strength and reactions. I spent another night at an ARVN firebase, but this time there was no ground attack after dark."

"I don't think anyone realized that I was now on Ranger South as there was no attempt to pick me up. When I was finally able to get on a slick (Note: Troop transport Huey) from Ranger South on the 22nd, the pilot did one of those departures that is like falling off a hill. I was afraid that we were going down and I yelled out loud, 'Oh, God, no!' I thought for sure we had been shot down, after all I had just gone through. But there were no shots fired, not even by the door gunners, and I think we flew right over the bad guys. I don't know why there were no shots. The 101st slick came in alone and we left alone, I didn't even see any gun ships."

"They took me to Camp Eagle and when we landed, a Cook met me with some sandwiches and cold milk. I didn't realize how hungry I was." Dennis was soon transferred to the 85th Evacuation Hospital at Phu Bai where he fully recovered from his wounds and was back on duty, fulfilling his obligation to Uncle Sam in Vietnam.

From the March 10, 1971, edition of the Honolulu Star Bulletin comes this article, which documents the missions of one of Fujii's Cobra rescue pilots, CWO Stephen M. Booker.

"On a mission one day Booker got instructions to contact 'Papa Whiskey' and was surprised to contact Fujii. 'There were not supposed to be any Americans on the ground operating in Laos. Later we found out he was a Crewchief of a medical evacuation helicopter, pinned down and under enemy ground attack, Booker explain.

He called air strikes dangerously close to his own position. It was due entirely to his efforts that the South Vietnamese elements on the ground were able to sustain the repeated communist attacks. The whole time he was there, the situation looked very grave. He was down in as perilous a position as anyone can be in, and came out of it.

The second time, my wingman got wounded in both arms and legs and needed medical evacuation back to the States. The third time, my aircraft suffered very heavy damage.

The pilots, who worked with him, like me, though we never met him, were deeply interested in his fate. One night word came that his position had been overrun and that he had been killed. It made us all depressed. Next day we learned he was alive. All of us pilots were pulling for him. He deserves a lot of respect.'

Booker spoke for all gunship pilots and praised the medical evacuation crews in their Dustoff helicopters.

'You cannot imagine how valuable of a service they perform to the elements on the ground.' He said. 'They fly the helicopters that go into the hottest areas in Vietnam, and elsewhere, to extract wounded soldiers.

The Dustoff people really are a dedicated lot. Often they save a life only to risk their own.'"

Final Author's note: For his actions during this and other missions, Dennis Fujii was awarded the Distinguished Service Cross, Silver Star, Purple Heart, two Air Medals, and Vietnamese Cross of Gallantry with Palm. He was also recommended for the Congressional Medal of Honor, but because his actions were "more of benefit" (my words) to the ARVNs than to the Americans, his award was denied. When Medic Geoffrey Morris heard that Fujii was being put in for the Medal of Honor, he had this to say to Fujii's Senator, the Honorable Senator Daniel K. Inouye of Hawaii:

October 29, 2003

Honorable Senator Daniel K. Inouye
722 Hart Building
Washington, DC 20510-1102
202-224-3934

RE: Dennis Mark Fujii
Dear Senator Inouye:

I have been advised that Dennis Mark Fujii is being considered for the Congressional Medal of Honor, and I have been requested to write to you concerning his past experiences with me in Vietnam.

From October, 1970 - February 15, 1971 I was paired with Dennis on a regular basis as a DMZ Dustoff Medic, which operated out of Quang Tri, Vietnam, approximately 10 miles from the DMZ. Our area of operations necessitated occasional trips into North Vietnam and Laos to recover downed pilots. It is ironic that I was supposed to have been the Medic with Dennis on the day his crew was shot down over Laos in early February 1971, and it was due to a last minute crew switch that resulted in my being replaced by another Medic.

I am certain that your research would indicate that our unit had an extremely high casualty rate, and although I don't remember the exact numbers, I know that well over half of our unit of approximately 32 pilots, Crew Chiefs, and Medics were killed over the course of my 14 month tour, with another six or seven going home early due to wounds received in action.

In all candor, I was truly blessed by virtue of the fact that I did not receive a scratch while in country, however, I am also mindful of the fact that I would not be here today if it wasn't for Dennis' quick response to an emergency situation that occurred during a hoist mission approximately two or three days before the event for which he has received so much recognition.

Page 2
October 29, 2003
Honorable Senator Daniel K. Inouye

Although the dates are a little bit fuzzy, I can recall that during the first week of February 1971, most of the missions were hot, and any venture into a landing zone was greeted with small arms fire, mortars, or recoilless rifle fire.

One particular event stands out in my mind, as our crew was returning from a hot mission only to receive an urgent May Day call from two pilots whose LOH or Cobra (I don't remember), had been brought down by enemy fire a few minutes before. They were in a real panic and the bad guys had surrounded their aircraft.

Although our helicopter was very low on fuel, the Aircraft Commander made a decision to attempt to extract these two men with a hoist. I remember standing on the skid while we were taking intermittent small arms fire from a considerable distance. We were able to retrieve the two pilots on a hoist when all of a sudden the hoist malfunctioned and started slipping in a downward position with the prongs open. This had never happened to me in my 14 months and I pushed the emergency switch; which, as you know, was supposed to fire a 45-caliber bullet severing the cable. That, too, malfunctioned so I was forced to attempt to pull the cable up from a distance of about thirty feet, hand over hand, with the attachments. At the same time, the pilot banked the aircraft stating he could wait no longer because we were dangerously low on fuel. I don't remember exactly what happened next other than for some reason the loose cable started unwinding and I was pulled out of the aircraft hanging on the skid with the cable wrapped around my right foot.

Dennis somehow managed to reach down and grab my clothing and hold me by the neck while I attempted to secure myself on the skid. We landed a short distance away and I cannot recall if we boarded another aircraft or managed to refuel by some other means.

I only know that I was surely saved from a 150-foot free fall by Dennis.

Simply stated, because of Dennis' quick actions, I've been given 33 additional years in which to marry a lovely lady and raise four children. It's ironic that he was shot down 72 hours later and I never had a chance to say good-bye. Although I wasn't with Dennis on the ground over there in Laos during that trying period, I am quite certain that his actions would have made any mother proud to have him as her son. I was honored to have Dennis as a friend and Crew Chief.

With kindest regards,

Geoffrey Morris

Mission 16

LOSS OF PILOT DEAN PEDINGS
AND
MEDIC DONALD WOODS

Looking for information, I put out an email to everyone in our database to try to determine who the Pilot-in-Command, PIC, was when we lost Dean Pedings and Donald Woods. Here was the reply that I received from Warrant Officer David Cole, a pilot who was with the 571st Medical detachment, Phu Bai Dustoff. Again, losses during Lam Son 719 were so high that assets of crews and helicopters were thrown together from 3 or 4 different units in I Corps.

Yes, I was the PIC on 15 Jun 71 when we were shot down on a hill, can't remember the name of it, along the southern edge of the Bai Long Valley, just east of FSB Sarge. We had picked up some RVN wounded and delivered them to the 18th Surgical Hospital in Quang Tri.

Warrant Officer Pilot David Cole

The US adviser on the ground had asked if we would come back to pick up their KIA's as he had not had any luck getting a slick to do so. I said ok and we returned to the LZ. We had to make three approaches due to weather and winds. On the third try while on the ground, the aircraft exploded and started bouncing down the side of the hill. I lowered the collective and when the aircraft came to rest, I looked to the right and saw Dean exiting the aircraft.

He appeared to have no apparent injuries and I didn't see any blood, and since he was exiting under his own power I assumed he was

OK. When I exited the aircraft, I looked in the back of the aircraft and all I saw was body bags.

The aircraft was burning at that point and the ammo we had on the aircraft was beginning to cook off so I moved up the hill and found the Crew Chief, can't remember his name, and he was badly wounded. He had been blown out of the aircraft due to the explosion. He said he remembered seeing a round come through the top of the aircraft and go through the floor before it exploded. Turned out it was an old French 75MM artillery round that got us. I guess they had the hill zeroed in and had time to set up on us during the three approaches.

The US adviser had already called in another Dustoff, Buddy Borders as a matter of fact, and they were in route. Since the aircraft was burning and the ammo was cooking off, I couldn't get to either Dean or the Medic. By the time Buddy Borders got there, the aircraft had pretty much burned down to a pile of metal and I scooped up the Crew Chief and carried him to Buddy's aircraft.

When we got to Buddy's aircraft, the other two did not show up and Buddy didn't want to sit there and have the same thing happen to him as happened to us, so we took off and orbited until the guys on the ground found the other two. As it happened, the explosion knocked two right transmission mounts loose, and the rotor system was tilted to the right.

Apparently Dean forgot to duck and caught a rotor blade in the head and that was what killed him. The Medic, his name was Donald Woods was apparently killed outright during the explosion.

Medic Donald Woods

He had 10 days to go in country and unfortunately had his dental records with him on the aircraft as he was going to get some work done on himself prior to going home. I was slightly wounded during this ordeal and spent about a week in the 18th Surgical Hospital, and another 3 weeks before I could get back to flying.

Pilot Dean Pedings

That was one of those experiences that I will never forget.

It seemed kind of ironic that Dean had been in country for a very short period of time and SP5 Wood had only a few days left before he was due to go home.

During that time, the 571st and the 237th were co-located at our home base of Phu Bai *and our field site was Quang Tri. SP5 Wood and I were in the 571st Dean was in the 237th I think, and I don't remember which unit the Crew Chief was in.*

I hope this helps Dean's family and anyone else who is interested. Please feel free to contact me if there is anything else I might be able to help with.

Pilot William "Buddy" Borders

With that same email request for information, I received this reply from Paul Simcoe, who was also involved with Joe Brown's death during Lam Son 719.

To protect the families, I have edited out some of the details. Here is his email:

Wow Phil! Dean Pedings! This is really strange. I have never been able to make it to the "Wall" in Washington, so a friend of mine's daughter just came back from there, having taken pictures of the names of some of my friends who didn't make it, and of course, Billy Dean Pedings is one of them. This is just a week ago, and now, here is a query about him from his family. Amazing.

We were good friends, over there. I was the Medic on the chopper that went out to find him after his bird got hit. They had landed on a ridge top; I don't remember which one, one of those really steep ridges on the way to Khe Sanh.

They apparently had already loaded some wounded, including ARVN and U.S., a Captain Dickey, I think Special Forces guy. My Crew Chief and I were just lolling about in the radio shack in Quang Tri, when we heard on the radio "Dustoff got hit." We ran to the tarmac, through the 18th Surg ER where we saw our pilots on the horn trying to get hold of us, so we all four ran straight out to our bird and took off.

By the time we got there, it just looked like a big torch on the ridge. I did not know if Dean's family would want to hear this. His chopper took a mortar hit directly on the right side, and burnt to death several wounded that were already on board, including Capt. Dickey. The awful thing is that the pilot; Lt. Cole, told me that he saw Dean struggle with the door handle just before he (the pilot) was able to bail. Pretty grim.

The pilot, Lt. Cole, survived with a few shrapnel wounds including a huge piece stuck in his neck that missed all vital structures. The Crew Chief was fairly new, I don't remember his name, was also peppered with shrapnel, but none of it life-threatening. Everybody on the right died, including the wounded; everybody on the left survived.

So, there was no trace whatsoever of Billy Dean Pedings, by the time we got there. I looked all over the place, especially around the right side, where it was basically already burnt to the ground, but there was nothing there, not even a helmet. Same with Donald Woods, the Medic. No body, no helmet, no uniforms, no weapons. (Ed. The remains were later recovered.)

I am really sorry that his family didn't hear from any of us about Dean; Dave Hansen was a good friend of his over there, and he might be a good source too. I thought Dean had a little girl at the time; you didn't hear anything about a daughter? Please let me know if any of his family wants to contact me. I'd be glad to talk to them, though I'll probably withhold some things.

Take care, Paul

Thus, our final two losses of crew-members and our final aircraft loss during 719.

Now the reader should have a better idea why Vietnam Veterans feel as they do about the war, and why it is so difficult for many to remember. As was mentioned before, War is <u>not</u> pretty!

Mission 17

Don't You Ever
Use My Call Sign Again!

Warrant Officer Joel Dozhier, DMZ Dustoff 713, arrived in country in 1970 and like virtually all of us, spent the first part of his year as a co-pilot, CP, and when he demonstrated his proficiency, was promoted to an Aircraft Commander, AC. His AC time in Vietnam included the infamous Lam Son 719 "rodent intercourse"... My words.

Over a beer or two, he tells about the time during 719 that so many friendly ARVN troops were hanging onto his Huey as he tried to leave an LZ, it was all he could do to get the aircraft a few feet into the air. Trying to obtain "translational lift", a point shortly after take-off at about 18 knots of air speed when the aircraft gains slightly more lift, Joel found himself staring at the top of a tank. It was all he could do to clear the tank by inches "but it knocked a few guys off the skids as I passed over the tank and that was enough to allow me to gain altitude. It wasn't intentional; it's just the way it worked out."

I believe that every one of us has our own "Boy, I wish I could have done that one over" story about our lives as Peter Pilots...Co-pilots. I know that I certainly have more than one! Joel's "call-sign" comment, the title of this mission, has a little background to it. The Co-pilot on this mission was a high time Co-pilot, meaning that he had just about paid his dues as the right-seater and was about ready to make the highly sought move to the left seat, the Aircraft Commander's position. During this time, ACs would let the co-pilots run the mission as if they were the AC so one could get acclimated to the big chair. On these transitional missions, the CP's would use the AC's call sign because that call sign was the one the men on the ground were told to expect. Such was the case for Warrant Officer Peter Pilot.

Warrant Officer Pilot Joel Dozhier

Joel says, "A couple days before the call sign incident, he and I were on a mission to Vandegriff, out near Laos. I always told my CPs 'Fly like you're gonna get shot at because you probably will.' So on the approach to Vandergriff, he does this low-level, 120-knot approach to the LZ, exactly like he was supposed to do. But as he's bringing the aircraft to a stop, he lets the aircraft balloon way high, maybe 150 or 200 feet, and there we are over the LZ with the guys on the ground looking straight up at us, a couple hundred feet over them! Roger 'Ramjet' Leseman, the crew chief, comes over the intercom and says, 'Tails clear, hoist going down!'

Crewchief Roger "Ramjet" Leseman, at right with helmet.

Of course, it was not a hoist mission, because by now they were supposed to be IN the LZ, not OVER it. Dozhier took over the controls and hovered the helicopter down to a safe landing, on the ground.

"Leseman was a character. There was an order put out that required a certain amount of military protocol at times. Roger took advantage of it in that whenever he would close my door before we took off, he would throw me a salute so I would have to salute him back."

The pick-up at Vandegriff was completed without incident and we move forward a few days to a return flight from Da Nang to Phu Bai. "I was letting the Co-pilot get some low level time as we headed back. He was getting pretty low over the water and kept getting lower, so I reminded him that the blue water can be deceptive and to bring it up a little, which he did. Then, as we started over the beach, I again felt he was too low and I told him that the white sand dunes were hard to distinguish at this altitude and maybe he should stay higher. After we cleared the beach, we're now inland over the trees. He was doing fine by now, but about a mile ahead of us, in a direct path to our front, was this big tree several feet higher than the others.

I'm watching him head straight for the tree and I'm thinking he's going to go left of it. Then I'm thinking, no, he's going to go right of it. Then it was, 'Thwack', he flew right into it! It caved in the battery cover and penetrated the chin bubble. As we approached Phu Bai, this Cobra pilot called us and tells us we have something hanging out of the aircraft and are we OK? Seems we have a big tree limb hanging out of the front of our helicopter! I told the Co-Pilot, 'Contact Phu Bai and use your call sign. Don't you ever use my call sign again!' And even the Tower tells us 'looks like you have something hanging from your helicopter.' Turns out we had several feet of tree sticking out of the nose. The limb was at least a couple inches in diameter."

And Joel also tells about the time he gave the 237th First Sergeant his last flight in Vietnam before returning stateside, "We took him out in the area and we're just flying around. We were low leveling down this river when he spotted this big lizard on the shore; it was 4 or 5 feet long. Someone decided it would be a good idea to shoot it, so we turned around and sure enough someone was able to kill it with their personal weapon. Then, the idea was hatched to pick it up, put it on a litter, and take it back to the hospital ER.

We landed on shore; the guys in the back loaded it and covered it up. We called in that we were returning with one patient. The crew delivered the litter to the doctors and nurses waiting in ER; my crew got a good laugh out of it when the cover was lifted!" I'm assuming the crew got all the laughs, not the doctors and nurses!

Such was the youth and humor of Dustoff crews in combat.

Mission 18

Black Bitch, UH-1H 66-01125, An insight into the personality of the most *infamous* DMZ Dustoff helicopter.

This was a "D" Model Huey converted to an "H" Model. Among other things, the H Models had the more powerful 1400 Shaft Horse Power, SHP, turbine engine rather than the 1100 SHP engine that came in the D Model. The story is narrated by Warrant Officer Pilot Gene George. Gene served in Vietnam from Nov 70 to Nov 71 and was a flight school classmate of David Hansen. Gene offered this story during the 2010 DMZ Dustoff reunion in Indianapolis:

"I want to talk about the worst helicopter in the unit. I was describing this war story yesterday, but Crewchief Jerry Graf confirmed it today. This aircraft really was a good aircraft, except when it heard one word. It had ears. Everybody liked to fly it until it heard the one word.

We had been flying all day, back hauling patients from Quang Tri (QT) to the 95th Evac (Evacuation Hospital) at Phu Bai.

Black Bitch with Mike Bradley in the right seat at the 18th Surgical Hospital pad, Quang Tri.

Late in the afternoon we were coming back and we heard a mission being called in to our RTO, Radio Telephone Operator. We let him know we were the closest aircraft and we would take the mission. As for the coordinates, we were only a couple of minutes away; we couldn't have been there any sooner if we had been in an F4. I took the information and the RTO said this *will* be a hot LZ. That's the magic word – HOT! That RTO no sooner got the words out of his mouth and I repeated it back, when caution lights started flashing!

The main problem was the main generator, which required immediate attention and we had to fly to QT without completing the mission.

As far as I know, they never found the problem with that generator; it was still working the next day. But I'm happy to know that she made it back to the States, where she continued to fly in the National Guard."

Mission 19

Jim Harris First DMZ Dustoff Hoist Mission

As I put out the call for stories of the 237th, Warrant Officer Jim Harris offered this installment of the first hoist mission flown by a 237th crew. Jim was one of the first Aircraft Commanders that I flew with and I have always had a lot of respect for him. After the war, he became a Missionary for his church. Here is his account,

Story by Jim L. Harris

"As I remember it, which in all honesty you must take in account my present age and fleeting brain cells... This is what and how it happened. The 237th was new in country and set up shop at Camp Evans under the leadership of Maj. Hull just North of the old provincial capital city of Hue. It was fall of 1968. I had graduated from Army flight school in July, class of 68-9, then immediately volunteered for Dustoff duty. So spent the month of August at Fort Sam getting my training as a Medical corpsman then in September arrived in Da Nang, Vietnam.

I was originally assigned to the 571st Med Detachment but after a month there was traded for a newby "Peter Pilot" from the 237th that had just arrived in country. The 237th needed experienced pilots to even out the tasks at hand thus the reason for the trade. I had recently made Aircraft Commander, which gave me the ability to command a Huey H model and its crew. I think the 571st was just responding to the letter of the law by making me Commander in order to keep their other experienced pilots. At any rate, here I was new in country and new to the 237th.

My first responsibility was assistant ops under Captain John Colvin. So we had a lot of "firsts" to work through in order to carry out our assignments and the tasks at hand. Eventually we knew we would get a request for a hoist mission, and finally it happened on my watch. It must have been late October or early November of that year when we had this mission come in late in the day.

Of course I don't remember the location except it was just West of our base. LZ Sword had artillery backup, which I planned on using if it became dark and the mission was still active. We were dispatched to the scene and found a likely spot for the extraction.

I picked a spot in between some high trees to settle the H-Model down below the tree line and dropped the Madaffer Jungle Penetrator or was it a wire basket? Told ya some cells were missing along with the data stored on them in my head. Oh well, back to the story. We had heard some shots ring out around us but the crew was very steady and kept their focus at the task at hand. No hits so far so it must have been ground fire. The crew chief and Medic did a good job of guiding our tail rotor through the branches in order to snug up into the treetops. The extraction took longer than we wanted and the sun was setting so we ordered illumination rounds from LZ Sword. We hovered fixed in one spot for a con-siderable amount of time. Longer than we wanted to I assure you. It felt like an hour, but had to be less... Maybe 45 minutes. I don't remember. But I had a good fix on a branch right in front of me so was able to hold the ship steady throughout the mission.

Finally the patient was loaded and on the rise from the triple canopy below. We didn't want any fancy stuff or heroics, just get the job done without incident and take our time working the tail rotor out of the trees. We climbed out of the position and headed home to the Evac Hospital to deliver our patient.

Put on a little fuel and flew back to the compound. Because of the time involved holding the ship in the trees, my legs were cramping a little so let the pilot fly back home. And then it happened. The only injury we received on this mission. Our own Cpt. Colvin perpetrated it. When we touched down in the revetment we had what seemed like the whole detachment there to welcome us home. And Cpt. Colvin opens my door for me laughing and excited that we pulled it off and and and and and... Ready for it? Slaps me on my left leg so hard I thought it was broken. I had a bruise there for over a week. I regret that I don't remember the names of my crew, but they did a tremendous job. We just tried to keep it textbook and it came off without a hitch. Except of course for my wounded leg."

Warrant Officers George Zuvela, L, and Jim Harris, R.

Mission 20

Major Gilliam

Medic Al "Doc" Jenkins, "Jinx" and I have become good friends since flying together with American Huey 369 the last few years. In Vietnam when we flew together, it was business, now it could be a lot more pleasure. We have kept up a rather busy email exchange and the subject of Major Frank Gilliam came up.

Major Gilliam was the replacement Commanding Officer, CO, of the 237th when the original CO, Major Don Hull, DEROSed home. I had the pleasure of flying with Major Gilliam only one time before going home myself, and it was a mission that we did not complete. It was not a combat mission, and the daytime weather was marginal. After about 15 minutes or so of flying to our objective, he decided to turn around due to the weather, and so, we returned to base at Camp Evans.

I'm sure my thought at the time was that we could have made it... Heck, he was a high time pilot and I was only days away from making Aircraft Commander. REAL helicopter pilots could have completed that mission!

But looking back, and being ABLE to look back, I know now that he made the right decision, especially since we later lost so many crew and aircraft to weather related accidents.

So to reinforce the "manly-hood" of Major Gilliam, Al Jenkins offered me these two tidbits of the new CO.   No one will ever accuse Jenkins of being an English major, as I am reproducing his emails <u>exactly</u> as he wrote them to me.   I offer the reader a glimpse of the Major through Al's eyes,

"Frank Gilliam took over Evans/DMZ DUSTOFF from Maj. Hull, our Daddy.   He seemed to young to be a Maj. and after Maj. Hull it couldn't get any better... But, the first time you flew with Frank you knew he had "DONE THAT had THE STUFF" all our ACs did. After one particular difficult mission, nasty LZ and a big load of wounded my mind told me "He's pretty damn good and "I'm coming home after this mess" and did.   I bet he can still shake a stick bettern' most.   I had a run in with a WO over a knife I carried, Peter Pilot took my knife!   Maj. Gilliam called me and Peter Pilot in and he said, "This knife has cut more boot laces than you can count" some times that's all you could do to prepare a guy for triage, gave me back my switch blade and told Peter Pilot to learn to fly, that's your job.

The crew will take care of the back. Man I was on cloud 9 and I knew this New, Young CO would run our Company well; he's a great friend too. Enjoy this mail."

Evans/DMZ DOC

"I think I told you about the time me and some other guys got busted at the Evans Gate while moving our stuff to Quang Tri. You won't believe this but we had illegal guns we had acquired when on standby at QT, illegal guns, ME, hard to believe I'd have an illegal gun. Anyway, we ended up at hundred and worst headquarters and they wanted to know who we were and what we were doing? We told the Capt of the Birds Nest we were the guys that pulled Real soldiers out of the ditch and we were called DUSTOFF. He had not a clue and Little Willie got pretty cocky with him so Capt. Stupid said, "Who's your CO?" Willie gave him our push and Capt. Stupid got on his Tonka Radio and called 706, Frank was in the air, as usual, and said he would refuel and fly down. He came in and read the riot act to Capt. Stupid, called the 101st names I never had heard. He said, "My men are leaving with me NOW" didn't get the guns back and we walked out to the bird without a word, I thought we were in deep shit.

So Maj. Gilliam spooled up the bird, hovered over the 101 MP Play Ground where they had a proper grill and tables and chairs, shade and all the good stuff. Frank pulled pitch and all I saw resembled a hurricane hitting their Recreation area. He never said another word and dropped us off at the Surg. went for fuel and never another word was said. Although we missed Maj. Hull we knew this Cowboy had us covered."

AL

Major Frank Gilliam,
The second Commanding Officer of DMZ Dustoff

Mission 21

My 1st Day
As An Aircraft Commander

Two parties shall remain nameless in this story. If you read this and want to know who they were, I will tell you verbally, but I will deny it under oath. Sadly, neither one is still with us.

I recently became reacquainted with the Medic in this story, Ellis Woodcock. Woodcock and I were talking about other members of the 237th and I related the incident to him; Ellis told me, "I was the Medic." I had forgotten it was him. Once again at the forefront of my memory, I decided I should put it on paper.

My first assignment as Aircraft Commander, AC, was 12 November 1969. It was an "Ash & Trash" mission to Red Beach at Da Nang. Ash and Trash meaning a Courier run, or parts run... Something of that order and certainly not combat time. The unnamed personnel were the co-pilot and the crew chief, both relatively new to flying on a daily basis. As far as the actual flying on this day was concerned, it was all perfectly normal; the "memorable" part comes on the way back at altitude.

About halfway back on the return flight, a few thousand feet high and well over "The Dead Man's Zone" (50 to 1500 feet, out of range of small arms fire), I noticed movement on the radio console. Out of the corner of my eye I saw Peter Pilot, the co-pilot, turn my transmitter selector switch to "Private" PVT. What the...??? Without saying anything, I simply reached over and turned it back to "1" with 1 being the FM radio position.

Normally we flew with the selector switch in 1 or 2 (VHF radio) so that at any moment of trouble, all we had to do was hit the transmit button on the cyclic stick to get out our message; no fumbling with the selector, it was already set. The transmitter selector switch determined which radio we transmitted on as opposed to the receiver switches which determined which radios we monitored. All of this was on the console between the pilot's seats. So I was a little miffed that he just reached over and changed my setting!

After I changed my transmitter switch back to 1, I watched him AGAIN turn it back to PVT. I was about to ask him what the Hell he was doing when I heard him say, "Crew Chief is too dumb to be flying."

He had also turned his switch to PVT and was initiating a conversation between just he and I without the guys in the back hearing us. Seeing that we were both on PVT, I replied, "Crew Chief is new, he's doing OK" or words to that effect. Peter Pilot replied with something like, "Well, I think he's too dumb to be a Crew Chief." Knowing I was still on PVT and knowing one just spoke into the microphone without touching anything, I again "stuck up" for Crew Chief, saying that I thought he was doing fine, and immediately moved my selector back to "1" conversation ended, or so I thought!

A couple hours after landing back at Evans, Peter Pilot and I were summoned to Major Donald Hull's office, our Commanding Officer. Again a, "What the...???" moment. He wanted to know about the conversation on the flight back from Da Nang. I'm thinking, "How did he know about that? Did Peter Pilot tell him about it? But then we wouldn't be down here. What the ...???"

Major Hull then related to us that the guys in the back were very upset about the conversation up front about Crew Chief. Then is dawned on me... The co-pilot in the right seat next to me was the Dumb Guy! Peter Pilot was also in PVT but was using his transmit button on the floor to talk to me!

I knew that all one had to do was talk... I was the experienced guy, but Funny New Guy and resident Peter Pilot was also transmitting his comments to the back by using his transmit button while in PVT! What a maroon! But what was so bad was that the guys in the back only heard Peter Pilot's negative comments and did not hear me sticking up for him because *I* knew how to use the intercom system!

I really felt badly about them hearing what was said up front, even though it was not my fault and I was not agreeing with Peter Pilot, but what really pissed me off was the fact that here I was, a brand new AC, something I had worked my butt off to get and I'm getting chewed out by the CO! It was a gentle chewing out, yes, but a dressing down, regardless. I don't know if Major Hull realized fully what had happened, if I was able to convey to him what went on, because I was also trying to have some decorum as Peter Pilot outranked me and I didn't want to call him an idiot in front of the CO. In fact, it may have taken me a few minutes to fully realize myself what had happened.

As it turned out, I never again had to fly with that Peter Pilot, but I did spend the entire rest of my flying in VN with Crew Chief.

And I will transmit now, for everyone to hear, that the Crew Chief in this story did an excellent job for me and I had complete faith in his ability to serve in that position. If he were alive today, I'd give him a big hug and tell him how much I enjoyed flying with him and also tell him that he was one of the best, "Charlie Echos" I ever flew with.

I miss him. He was a good guy. He deserved better.

Specialist Ellis Woodcock, Medic

Mission 22

"I'm The Pilot"
Phil Marshall, Ed Paradis
Don Study, David Reeves

Sgt. Ed Paradis

13 November 1969 Sgt. Ed Paradis of the 101st Airborne Division "Screaming Eagles" was enjoying the rare luxury of a little Rest & Relaxation at China Beach, South Vietnam. A combat veteran of several months, he was glad for the break that he felt he deserved. But it was not to last; a "Red Alert" came down from headquarters.

An Armored Personnel Carrier (APC) and an OH-6 Army Light Observation Helicopter (LOH) were lost near the Demilitarized Zone. There was nothing to be found of either of these vehicles that were assigned to the 5th Mechanized Brigade near Quang Tri. "They told us that the helicopter was blown out of the sky and it was if they all had fallen off the face of the earth."

Ed and the other troopers in his unit were told to prepare themselves well and not to forget any equipment. They would be going up against highly trained North Vietnamese regulars, and they would be "playing in their yard, not ours!" Twelve hours later, the sky was filled with Huey and Chinook helicopters as they were flown from Da Nang to Camp Eagle; headquarters of the 101st Airborne. The two-hour flight was more than enough for Ed to think about what was going to happen.

A Special Forces unit had picked out and cleared the landing zone, and as the sky troopers landed to begin their sweep of the area, the Special Forces advance team departed the area on the Huey transports that had brought in Ed Paradis and his buddies. "You could look in any direction and see fully loaded American troops of the 101st!" Ed recalled later, "These guys were ready for some heavy stuff. You knew that it wasn't going to be a walk in the park!"

14 November 1800 Hours. They started their sweep that evening and headed north. They stopped at the top of a hill for the night, and cleared out 45-degree fire zones for their foxholes. Ed was cutting elephant grass in front of his hole with his machete when he heard a "pop" go by his ear. He casually brushed it off and continued swinging his knife when some one yelled, "Get down, you stupid SOB!" He turned around in time to see a single enemy troop in a tree taking shots at them! They lobbed over 20 rounds of M-79 grenades at him and he casually watched the rounds explode all around him. Apparently tiring of the show, the enemy trooper slung his AK-47 over his shoulder and jumped down out of the tree, disappearing into the woods and was gone!

15 November 1969. The following morning, they arose early and were on their way at daybreak. They continued their sweep, until about 11:00 AM when they again came under fire from an NVA regular, this time a soldier in full uniform. He fired from a shallow position known as a "spider hole;" he was a hard-core sniper and it took almost 30 minutes before Ed and his comrades could silence this dedicated man. They continued, "humping the boonies" until later that afternoon when they found the wreckage of the helicopter. One crewman was found dead, but strangely, he had been bandaged and was on a stretcher!

No evidence of the other crewman or APC was found, nor was there any track marks from the carrier; but here was this approximately 19 year old crewmember lying on a stretcher.

Ed normally kept himself distant from the casualties of war, but this time he had to make an exception. This helicopter crewman had been wounded several times, but was still alive at some point after the crash.

Yet the North Vietnamese did not allow him to live. A pocket Bible was found in his flight helmet, and in the Bible was an inscription from his mother; "May God watch over you and bring you home safe." Ed felt his insides turn and his heart went out to this young red headed helicopter crewman and his family, for the first time since his tour started, Ed knew what it was like to hate. Always before it was just a job; now he knew what it was like. This would turn out to be the only bit of wreckage or remains that they found during the sweep that they were directed to make.

With the removal of the body, they received new orders.

A series of three depressions (saddles) along a ridgeline nearby were thought to contain a radio position and mortar firing points. Volunteers were needed to check out the area and Ed's squad, call sign "Click 66" decided that they would go. Helicopters were called in to transport them and they were lifted to a position approximately 3 kilometers from the area to be scouted.

By now it was 3:00 in the afternoon when they dropped their rucksacks and hid them near the trail, taking only essential survival gear, radio, weapons and ammunition. The squad of fourteen men was split into two groups, and Sgt. Paradis hand signaled the M60 machine gunner to follow his group up the hill while the others waited in the valley. Unfortunately, the gunner misunderstood and stayed below, greatly diminishing the firepower they would very soon need.

At a break in the foliage overlooking the first saddle, Sgt. Paradis and his buddy Sgt. Mueller were taken aback when they immediately were able to count 37 bunkers with more surely hidden all around the area. Movement was seen around most of them and it was obvious that they were in the middle of a very large concentration of enemy troops!

Suddenly, an NVA soldier was spotted nearby to their left and then just as quickly, he dropped to the ground and began to crawl to the closest bunker, which was only about 25 feet away.

Paradis and Mueller looked at each other and couldn't decide whether the enemy soldier had spotted them or not. They decided that they could not let him warn the others where they were, so it was left to the best marksman in the unit to stop him. "He could drive a 10 penny nail at a hundred yards." "We told the kid to take him out," Ed later recalled. The NVA was only two or three feet from the bunker when an accurate round from the MI6 struck him in the head, stopping him instantly.

But to the amazement of the US troopers, two hands reached out of the bunker to drag in the apparently dead soldier. The marksman again took aim, this time striking his target in the wrist. "I know that guy had to pull back a stump; I can still see that hand clutching its buddy's shoulder, but there was no arm attached to it!" Hearing the commotion at the top, the commanding officer wanted to know what was going on, and upon being appraised of the situation, they were ordered to take out the bunker.

Mueller and Paradis didn't say a word to each other, and before they realized it, they were within 5 feet of the enemy bunker. They finally looked at each other and Paradis said, "What are we doing here?" and Mueller responded, "I don't know but you'd better throw a grenade!"

Sgt. Paradis removed a grenade, pulled the pin… It seemed like 5 minutes - and tossed it at the opening.

Incredibly, it hit a pole that was sitting on the back of the bunker, and bounced back towards them! Paradis looked at Mueller, Mueller looked at Paradis and said, "Oh, F***!" and they turned on their sides and tensed their muscles to reduce penetration of shrapnel. The grenade exploded and incredibly, neither soldier got a scratch. Ed reached for another grenade -he knew he had 6 more - and they were gone! They apparently had fallen off while they crawled down the hill. He yelled to the top of the hill for another grenade and Allen Grotzke tossed one down. Paradise again pulled the pin, but this time he let it "cook off" for two seconds before releasing it.

His thought was, "God be with me" as he let it roll out of his hand towards the bunker.

Two sets of hands came out of the bunker as it got there, but they were not quick enough nor were the North Vietnamese screams effective enough to stop the technology of an American made grenade.

With the explosion of the bunker, it was if everything stood still. The dust rose and the entire bunker collapsed. And that's when the sky fell in, Ed recalled later. The whole area immediately opened up from machine gun fire and small arms fire in all directions except immediately above them where the rest of the squad was. Mueller had his M16 in his hand and was returning fire while Paradis reached for his weapon to his right.

They received supporting fire from above and Ed was preparing to fire when he felt a slight burning sensation in his right leg. Oddly, he had been looking down hill, but now with the burning sensation, he had been spun 90 degrees to the right while sitting!

At that time Mueller called out, "My God, I'm hit!" As Paradis turned to look, he could see the ball joint of Mueller's left shoulder exposed as he reached to feel the loose skin of the wound; it looked as if someone had taken a knife and cut it open.

Mueller began to run up the hill and Paradis moved to follow. As he put his hand on a log to push himself up, he felt a warmth and saw blood.

He put his hand to his calf and again saw nothing but blood. He thought, "I'm hit, too!" but he didn't try to run.

Grotzke, next in command of those still on the hill, started down, yelling, "I'm coming to get you!" Paradis waved him back. Ed felt that it was too dangerous for Grotzke to try, and for some reason, he didn't think this was his time to die; he didn't want someone else to get hurt trying to help him.

As Ed glanced to his left, he saw an NVA soldier pointing the muzzle of his weapon up the hill. Paradis looked up at his buddies just in time to see Grotzke grab his chest. The same enemy soldier who had shot the first two had now taken aim and fired again.

Ed saw Allen take 3 or 4 gulps of air and then fall forward. For the second time in his life, and for the second time that day, Ed Paradis hated.

The enemy soldier who had apparently wounded all three was now the only thing on the mind of Sgt. Paradis. The adrenalin was flowing as hard as it could pump as Ed took a nearly full clip out of his weapon, methodically inserted a full one, chambered the round, and took dead aim at the enemy soldier's belt buckle. "I looked at his face; he couldn't have been more than 17. And here he was with a 37 Caliber weapon, shooting us up."

Ed very deliberately flipped the M16 to semi-automatic and emptied all 18 rounds into his victim, the last round striking the enemy in the forehead. From the time the first round hit the buckle until the last round hit the head and the young soldier let go of his weapon and fell to the ground, everything went in slow motion for Ed.

Only after his immediate mission was accomplished did Ed Paradis run to save himself with the rest of his squad. Now reunited, Mueller asked him if he was hit and Ed showed him his mangled leg with parts of the calf in places where it wasn't supposed to be. "Yeah, I guess you did!" was Mueller's comment.

15 November 1700 Hours. Temporarily out of sight of the enemy, the squad regrouped and the Second Lieutenant commanding officer threw Ed Paradis over his shoulder in the traditional fireman's carry. Having retreated to relative safety, they had time to gather their thoughts and realized that they were in the middle of a very large concentration of enemy troops. They were still in deep trouble. Continuing to evade the enemy, they were able to secure a position on the side of a hill; an area that had been napalmed and with 4 to 5 foot high stumps. It was certainly a less than ideal area for a Medical evacuation helicopter to rescue wounded men. Sgts. Mueller and Paradis took turns working on Grotzke; as one tired, the other took over.

1930 Hours, 15 November.   U.S. Army Warrant Officer Phil Marshall, a 21 year old Medical evacuation helicopter pilot from Ohio, began to write in his diary, just as he had every evening before going to bed for the past 4 and 1/2 months. He was con-cerned about the enemy activity near the Demili-tarized Zone (DMZ) that was part of the area his 237th Medical Detachment was responsible for in South Vietnam.

So far this day, the crew had worked together as well as any group of 4 men who had been together for months; but these men had only flown together for hours.

A hoist mission earlier in the day, the most dangerous of all Medevac missions, had bonded them already. UH-1 "Huey" helicopters have the ability to electrically hoist troops up to 300 feet through trees and heavy jungle when the terrain does not allow the aircraft to land. However, this leaves the crew and aircraft extremely susceptible to enemy fire; the proverbial "sitting ducks" as the helicopter hangs in mid-air. But they were able to complete the rescue and save a life as the ground soldiers provided covering fire into a bunker complex only 50 yards from the pilot's left shoulder.

Phil's thoughts to his diary started off with, "All hell broke loose today, my first day as Aircraft Commander in Quang Tri.

A hot hoist mission and all of our pickups tonight and this afternoon were fragment wounds and RPG's (Rifle Propelled Grenades)..." and ended with "...it should be pretty quiet the rest of the night; at least I hope so. Tonight I'll say my prayers." He put down his pen, turned off the single bare bulb that hung high in the rafters of the plywood hooch that served as their temporary quarters and crawled under the mosquito net hoping to get 8 hours of sleep, a rare luxury in a combat zone. But in the back of his mind, he knew that Medevac aircraft were often called out into the night to rescue wounded soldiers.

What he didn't know was that at that very moment, there were already three "grunts" in need of his helicopter, his crew and their expertise.

1945 Hours. "Why can't we get a Medevac in here?" was the question. "It's too dangerous right now!" was the answer, but the Medic and radio operator were relentless. "Tell those gunships that if they don't get a Dustoff out here right away, we're going to open up on them ourselves!" "We've gotta get these guys outta here. It's been too long already. We have to find an LZ for Dustoff!" Every time a flare went off, Ed would look 50 meters away and see the reflection of enemy helmets moving in the dark. Whether it was the truth or whether it was to calm them down, he didn't know, but they told them a Dustoff was on the way. He knew that if they didn't get off the hill soon they were "dead meat."

1951 Hours. Phil could hear the running footsteps on the wooden walkway; the radio operator was on a dead run with an "Urgent" Dustoff mission. "Dustoff" was the call sign given to Army Helicopter Ambulances. The mere mention of the word and the distinctive sound of the approaching rotor blades was a definite boost to an injured soldier's morale. Instantly awake, the rest of the crew ran to the aircraft while Phil headed for the radio shack to get the mission sheet with the pickup coordinates, unit radio frequency and other information they would need to attempt the rescue.

Helicopter crews "almost never" refused a Medevac; they knew that lives and families at home depended on them to do their job, risky as it might be.

349

The information on the sheet was not good; three seriously wounded soldiers, including one with a critical chest wound. Phil ran to the aircraft, tucking the paper into his breast pocket where it joined a letter he had received that evening from his girlfriend and had only been able to read 3 or 4 times – so far. He began to buckle into the left seat as a call of "Clear!" from the 23 year old Co-Pilot Don Study from Indiana let everyone know he was "pulling the trigger" to start the turbine engine. The Crew Chief and Medic immediately echoed his "Clear!" with their own to indicate to Don they were ready and it was safe to start the aircraft.

With his helmet on, his .38 caliber handgun for personal defense repositioned between his legs for additional protection of the "vital" parts and his armor secured in front of his chest, Phil now took control of the aircraft. As the UH-1 "Huey" continued to run up, Don began buckling himself up and hurriedly finished preparing for what would prove to be a very "memorable" flight.

This entire procedure generally took less than three minutes from radio call to take-off. While on field standby as they were this night, the crew was totally independent with no back up crews or any other support from maintenance.

Even other crews not on duty would be welcome support as the camaraderie and bonds among them were as strong as any combat troops have ever experienced, perhaps because they faced death on a daily basis. Often, a pilot would run for an aircraft on an urgent mission, only to hear another pilot call after him "If you don't make it back can I have your fan?" Phil had the only popcorn popper in the unit, so he often heard them ask for his popper instead of his fan, both valuable commodities in Southeast Asia. It made him feel good and he laughed when they did this bit of macabre pilot humor; he knew that when they called after him like that, it was because they cared about him.

1954 Hours. As they got light on the skids, Don called for takeoff clearance from Quang Tri tower. Approval was always quick for a Dustoff helicopter on an urgent mission and Phil continued to climb out as the tower cleared them for take-off. He stayed low until beyond the traffic pattern and other air traffic in the area. The Co-Pilot now called the artillery support center to find out where they were firing from and where the rounds were impacting. Helicopter crews used this information to fly around or under artillery fire; a round through the cargo compartment could ruin your day! As the information was coming back over the radio, Phil noticed the dim glow of flares on the northern horizon. He didn't have to look at his map; he now knew exactly where they were going. They would be within a mile of North Vietnam!

1959 Hours. Arriving in the area of the wounded, Phil saw several aircraft and several landing zones (LZs) marked with strobe lights in the flare-brightened expanse of mountains and foothills. A radio call to the gunships circling the area brought a response of "I'll make a low pass over your LZ with flashing position lights." Some confusion developed because of all the activity and Dustoff 711, Phil's call sign, was directed by the gunship pilots to the wrong LZ. Immediately upon touching down, troopers tried to load crates onto the aircraft, and 19 year old Specialist Fourth Class Zettie (Zeb) Dulin, also from Indiana, shouted into the intercom "They're trying to load ammo; we're in the wrong LZ!"

At that instant, movement out the left window caught Phil's eye; another Huey was inbound on short final for the same LZ, and Phil was sitting where they wanted to land! "Comin' up!" Phil shouted back into the intercom. This alerted the crew that they were taking off as he pulled power into the rotor system to quickly leave the landing area. Helicopter crews did not like to be sitting on the ground in combat areas because they were very easy and tempting targets. It was bad enough going into a hot LZ when one had to, frightening when the pilot was in the wrong one!

Adrenalin was quickly pumping through each of the crewmembers.

Back to the FM radio with Click 66 on the ground, Phil told the RTO, Radio Telephone Operator, to turn off his strobe light. "Turn it back on" Phil next told them.

"OK, turn it back off" and with this quick exchange, Phil and Don were able to insure the correct LZ. Finally, with a "Turn it back on, I've got you." Phil was finally able to locate the blasted out hillside where the wounded lay; they were on the extreme north-western edge of the lighted area. Tall tree stumps lined the bomb cratered area where the wounded lay as Phil was finally able to approach the correct LZ. But now a new problem arose; he could not land in the area. He would have to hover as low as the defoliated trees and whirling rotor blades would allow him and hope that it was enough.

Fortunately it was, but the troops on the ground had to lift the wounded several feet into the open cargo compartment of the hovering Huey, taxing the abilities of the entire crew and also those on the ground.

2002 Hours. Paradis, Mueller, Grotzke and the others heard the tell tale, "whop-whop-whop" of the Huey's rotor blades closing in on their LZ. The red cross on the nose, doors and belly left no doubt as to the mission of this aircraft and the wounded soldier in the field knew that helicopter crews would take many risks to save the lives of others.

Ed suddenly became very concerned; when the helicopter pilot turned on his landing light at the last possible second, it reflected off enemy helmets like ants on an anthill. Ed knew that this pilot either didn't know what he was getting into, or if he did, he was a real "bonehead!"

As the wounded were lifted on board the aircraft, the last man in, Paradis, took a sitting position on the floor of the cargo compartment against the rear bulkhead and behind the left pilot's seat. He knew that they were not "out of the woods" yet!

2003 Hours. Helicopter pilots soon learned that there was an almost "fail-safe" way to know when wounded were loaded on board their aircraft without even looking. There is a very distinctive odor when jungle, sweat, blood and burned gunpowder are all mixed together; a fragrance that Dustoff crews especially never forget.

Just like the distinctive smell of body bags, a whiff of anything similar today whisks them back decades to those adrenalin-filled times of their lives. As the third (and last) trooper was lifted in, Specialist Fourth Class David Reeves, a 21 year old Medic that had a "safe" job in a secure hospital but wanted to fly, cried out, "We're up!" the signal that they were loaded and ready to go.

Immediately Reeves began caring for the worst of the three wounded, the chest wound of Grotzke. Reeves saw that he had a gross opening; which exposed his right chest cavity. His field dressing and plastic chest seal had come off, probably as he was being lifted into the Huey. Reeves felt no carotid pulses (damn gloves) but Grotzke moved when Reeves touched him.

After hearing Reeves' "Were up!" and without hesitation, Phil again began to lift off from a hostile landing zone. Most Dustoff pilots in Phil's unit subscribed to the theory that if you got into an LZ from a certain direction without taking fire; you should also leave in that direction. However, the North Vietnamese and Viet Cong believed in another theory: When you see a helicopter with red crosses coming in, let them get in and load more souls on board before you open fire as they come out!

Horrified, Paradis saw the pilot bank the aircraft to the left, taking them dangerously close to the enemy bunkers. He and Mueller exchanged fitful glances, knowing what was there. No one had told Phil Marshall where the enemy was hiding and in the confusion of finding the right LZ, he was unsure of just exactly where he was. There was no supporting fire from the ground troops and none from the gunships in the air. They were all alone; seven souls in an unarmed helicopter against a full regiment of NVA troops.

Ed tried to tell the Crew Chief, "Don't let him turn that way!" but the din of the aircraft and the crewman's helmet didn't allow Ed to be understood. He scrambled to the pilot's seat, tapped him on the shoulder and said, "Don't go over that hill!"

It was too late... Unfortunately for Phil and the other 6 men on board, the North Vietnamese theory took precedence.

A full clip of 30 rounds was fired from a Communist AK-47 assault rifle at the Huey with the last round penetrating the thin aluminum skin of the pilot's door. The armored seat stopped the initial trajectory of the bullet, but not the shrapnel from the seat itself and what was left of the round as it shattered. Hot metal fragments ripped into the bottom of Phil's left arm, severing the ulnar nerve and causing his now numbed hand and arm to be jerked off of the controls. He unwittingly rolled off the throttle as his arm flew up from the impact.

Red warning lights on the instrument panel immediately began glowing and the low RPM audio began to blare in both pilot's headsets. Rotor speed, which keeps the helicopter in the air and the rotor blades intact, began to get critically low. Being only 2 or 3 hundred feet off the ground, impact was imminent but the two pilots were not about to give up. With a call of, "I'm hit! I'm hit!" Phil let his Co-Pilot Warrant Officer Study know that he was in trouble.

Don grabbed the controls, and feeling that the throttle was loose, rolled it back on. At that same instant, with his right hand Phil flipped his radio to the gunship frequency and got out a transmission, "Mayday... Dustoff 7-1-1... I'm hit and going down!" Standard procedure was to repeat the word, "Mayday" 3 times, but they were so close to crashing, he felt that if he repeated it 3 times, he would not have time to get out the rest of his transmission. His hope was that someone might survive this inevitable crash; then he thought to himself, "This is it, Phil!" His next thought was to wonder how his family back home would take the news of his death.

Centrifugal force is the law of physics that keeps a helicopter's blades flat and intact. If a helicopter's blades slow down in flight, however, as happened when the throttle was rolled off when Phil was hit, the blades begin to bend upward and if the rotor system is not quickly brought back up to flight RPM, the blades will literally break away from the helicopter as they "cone" upward.

It only takes a very few seconds for this to happen and Phil knew it. Although later visual inspection of the blades showed major stress due to the coning as they fell out of the air, the helicopter flew smoothly. The aircraft would not be flown again until the damaged blades were replaced. In fact, when the blades were tied down later the next day for aircraft recovery, the tip of one of them broke off!

Surprisingly, however, all the gauges began to come back up "to green" as Don rolled on throttle and power returned to the engine. But they were still heading for the ground! Phil got back on the controls and together, the two pilots pulled the falling ship out of this certain fatal dive, so close to crashing that they clipped treetops with the rotor blades as they began their climb out to somewhat safer altitude.

Through the open door of the cargo compartment, Ed saw the green tracers and heard the round hit the aircraft; he saw the pilot's arm fly up into the air and he thought, "We're goin' down!" as they started to fall towards the jungle hillside. He heard Specialist Dulin, the Crew Chief yell, "He's hit!"

Ed thought, in his words, "We were in a world of s..t!" But something right finally happened and Ed saw the pilots doing what they were trained to do; reacting properly in an emergency situation. Once again under control, the aircrew could set about the task of tending to their passengers.

On the way out of the area, the Medic and Crew Chief did what they could for the wounded. Ed prayed for Allen's life.

2004 Hours. Things now appeared under control. The instruments remained in the green since recovering from the dive. Zeb was on the mike telling Reeves that the pilot was hit.

Not until that time did Reeves understand that Marshall was wounded. He was so preoccupied with his patient that he failed to realize that a guy up front was also hurt. The Huey of flying wounded headed East towards the South China Sea.

Aware that he was bleeding from his forearm, but not knowing the extent of the wound, Phil asked Reeves for a bandage. Without tying the bandage in place, Phil simply placed the bandage under his arm and held it in place against his upper thigh as they continued from the combat area. A Command and Control helicopter, callsign "Batman" flew behind Phil to insure they were OK. Quick communication from Phil let Batman know the extent of his injuries and that everything else was "in the green."

During this time, Reeves continued his work on Grotzke. He resealed the opening with his torn field dressing and plastic, rolled him back onto his right chest applying enough pressure to keep the open chest wound closed for the flight back.

Reeves tried to talk to Allen later on during the flight but there were no significant responses other than minimal movements. Allen Grotzke was in great stress.

Medic David Reeves

Phil commented to Don, the copilot, "I'm feeling a little light headed but I'll keep working the radios while you fly." Without saying another word to Phil, WO1 Study barked on the intercom to the Crew Chief, "Zeb, red handle that mother!" Before Phil had the chance to say anything, the Crew Chief yanked the red handles that locked the armored seat in position and Phil found himself still strapped to the seat but now looking at the roof of the cargo compartment! Unbeknownst to the flight crew, Ed Paradis' injured leg was pinned under the heavy armored seat and Ed was not too happy about this!

Unable to reach either the floor button intercom switch or the cyclic mounted button, Phil was able to finally make his wishes known over the noise of the aircraft by motioning and shouting as loudly as he could, "I'm alright, put me back up!" which Zeb promptly did, much to Ed Paradis' relief! However, Zeb failed to relock the red handles.

2005 Hours. At the Quang Tri Dustoff radio room, Callsign, "Glossy Pinner" the RTO has been monitoring Dustoff 711's mission, as was part of Standard Operating Procedure, SOP. To his horror, he realized that Phil had taken fire and was wounded.

His reaction was to call 237th Headquarters at Camp Evans and let them know what had just happened. Upon receipt of the message, the word immediately went out to the other pilots and crews at Evans; Phil was wounded and in trouble. Soon, most the men of the 237th were hanging around the radio room, listening to the radios to find out what was going on. Talk was in hushed tones so that no one spoke too loudly, for fear of drowning out the radios. They were very concerned about "one of their own." Occasionally hearing Phil's voice gave them some relief that at least he was still able to use the radios and they were still in the air.

2015 Hours. A call from Phil to the hospital ship "Repose" notified the trauma team of the nature of the wounded on board, including Grotzke's critical condition. "I guess I'll be spending some time with you tonight, too. I've been wounded in the arm," he also told the radio operator. "Understand you are wounded also?" came the surprised reply. Phil's answer was short. "Roger that!"

In the back of the Huey, work continued on Grotzke. Unfortunately, CPR was out of the question with such an open chest wound and starting an IV with only the red light was beyond Reeves skill level. Despite everyone's best efforts, Allen Grotzke did not survive.

Reeves felt that he probably lost him shortly before they landed on the ship.

2020 Hours. One of the most difficult things for any pilot to do is land on a ship at night, be it a jet on an Aircraft Carrier or a helicopter on a hospital ship. The Repose in sight, Phil grew concerned, not only because as the Aircraft Commander he was not able to control the aircraft with no feeling in his left hand, but as a new Co-Pilot, Don Study was far from experienced at landing on the pitching deck at night. Only a few short months before, Phil had made his first attempt at landing to the ship at night.

As a new Co-Pilot, the Aircraft Commander allowed Phil to "get his feet wet" at landing on a postage stamp as the Navy calls it. During the day, using depth perception to "home in" on the ship was like any other approach, but at night, the pilots were looking at virtually a single light in a sea of stark darkness and depth perception was practically nil.

Phil's first attempt on his own those months ago resulted in the aircraft terminating at a hover about 30 feet over the deck, and no place to go but straight down.

NOT the way to land on the ship, and the Aircraft Commander, knowing that Phil would probably need help on this first attempt, keyed his microphone and calmly said, "I've got it" and then muscled the Huey down to a very unorthodox landing.

All this was going through Phil's mind as they got closer and closer to the deck, or as Phil would call it years later, the corner of a postage stamp. If Don got in trouble during short final, they were all in a world of "sugar." But drawing on all his abilities, Don made an excellent approach and landing to the ship; flying skillfully all the way down to the darkened deck, a deck darkened so as not to blind the pilots and crew when landing. The new Co-Pilot carried it all the way down to a light in the middle of nowhere.

Immediately upon touchdown, intense floodlights were lit, greeting the Medevac helicopter and the 7 men on board. Phil was surprised to see so many people witnessing their arrival. Late night landings were usually only met with the mandatory landing personnel. However, this time, there were approximately 50 people lining the deck including a funny looking guy completely dressed in a silver suit holding a fire hose! The landing safety officer, LSO, ran to the left door of the Huey.

Earlier that day, Phil and his crew had brought patients to the hospital ship.

As often happened, the LSO would chat with the AC until it was time to leave. That afternoon, the last thing the LSO said to Phil was, "I hope I don't see you anymore today" knowing that the fighting had intensified.

Now, sitting on the deck again, the LSO opened Phil's door and said, "Damn it, I said I didn't want to see you again today!"

With his patients now unloaded from his aircraft, and with those 51 people watching through the windshield, Phil released his seat belt and "chicken plate" armor and threw his leg over the cyclic to climb out of the aircraft.

But instead of gracefully leaving the airplane, by shifting his weight against the back of the seat (with the red handles still unlocked), he promptly fell backwards into the cargo compartment! The safety officer helped him back up in the seat as a sheepish grin crept over Phil's face. He looked over at Don Study and said, "That's one you owe me! See you guys later." And still holding the bandage in place with his right hand, Phil climbed out of the cockpit with the LSOs assistance. He then headed for the ER, a corpsman supporting him as they walked.

2025 Hours. In the emergency room of the ship, Phil learned that one of the troops had died on the way in, but the others should be fine. He spoke briefly to one of the two surviving soldiers... He introduced himself to Phil as Eddie and when he realized that Phil was the pilot, he told Phil that he loved him!

Phil replied, "Not here, someone might see us!" And then they laughed the laugh of those that have just cheated death.

2100 Hours. At Camp Evans, Headquarters of the 237th Medical Detachment, it was determined that Phil was safely on board the Repose and the rest of the crew was safely back on the ground.

All the 237th officers and crewmen were invited to the Officer's Club for an "impromptu" get-together to discuss what had happened. 18th Surg Doctors and Nurses were also present when the crew of 7-1-1, without Marshall, showed up to relate the night's events.

Saturday Morning, Beavercreek, Ohio, November 15th. As was her habit, whenever Phil's Mother, Lois Marshall, sent a package to him, she made a note on her calendar as to the contents so she could let Phil know what to expect. On this morning as she sat at her desk, for the only time during Phil's tour so far, she made a note on this date: "I'm worried about Phillip." Because of the 12-hour difference in time zones, it was Saturday night in Vietnam when it was Saturday morning in Beavercreek. Later, as best they could tell, they determined that Lois wrote the note at the exact moment that Phil was falling out of the sky and wondering how his family at home would take his death. Of course, Lois had no idea what has just happened to her only son.

1600 Hours, Beavercreek, November 17th 1969. Phil's parents, Lois and Whitey, arrive home mid-afternoon from their "Mom & Pop" restaurant, the Beaver Grill.

Another tiring day but they enjoy the camaraderie and good-natured bantering of the customers and friends each day around the "Liar's Table." A large, 10 place table, it's where many of the local citizens enjoy discussing both world events and everyday life. As they approach the door to their home, they see a note... A note from Western Union that they have a telegram but they must telephone a number first to receive it. Knowing the possible meaning of a telegram while their son is in Vietnam, they hastily call the number to learn the contents of the message, but the voice on the other end is not permitted to read them the telegram, it must be delivered in person. Assured that it will be sent out immediately, they sit down and wait, pondering the contents of the yellow envelope that they will have to read soon. Wanting to know... But NOT wanting to know, also.

1630 Hours. The driver arrives with the envelope, and it's the proverbial "bad news, good news" message. Phillip is wounded but it is not life threatening and he will be coming home. The balance of the telegram was that there would be no more messages from the Army, so expect to hear from your son next.

Noon, November 24th. It has now been a week since the telegram arrived and no word yet from Phil to his parents. Mail from Phil normally took a week, but everyone was hoping for something sooner.

Sitting at the Liar's Table at lunch, Bud Walker, a regular customer at the Grill and a Post Office Carrier, shares the other's concerns at the table about the lack of news. Phil was often the topic of conversation to Whitey and Lois with almost daily inquiries from many customers as to how he was doing in Vietnam. Bud decided to do something about the situation. After completing his daily deliveries, he arrived back at the Xenia Post Office and went straight to the mail that had just come in that afternoon. Sifting through the hundreds and thousands of letters, he found the prize he was looking for, a letter from Phil. He called the Marshall's and told them what he found and let them know it would be waiting for them at the front window of the Post Office. Nothing would stop THIS carrier from his duties, even as he went "above and beyond."

Phil's letter let them know that he was OK and that the Doctors told him he would be home by Christmas. With a few details of the incident, he went on to tell them not to worry, everything would be fine and that he would be in touch again soon. Whitey and Lois could now resume their "normal" lives.

1300 Hours, March 20, 1970. It's been over 3 months since he was wounded and Phil has just received his personal belongings that were packed for him by the other pilots when he didn't return from his last mission.

As he slowly went through the large wooden crate, he mentally inventoried the clothes and other memorabilia. "It's all here," he thought, "even my diary." But then he realized that something was missing... His popcorn popper! He didn't make it back and they kept his popper! He smiled to himself and he felt good. They were more than welcome to it and he was glad they had it; hopefully they would remember him each time they used it! Years later, he found out that indeed, it had been put to VERY good use in his absence!

July 1989. Washington DC 20 Years later. While at the Vietnam Veterans Memorial, The Wall, Phil searched for the panel that displayed the names of those lost on November 15th 1969. He felt that the reason he was able to survive the war was because he went out on that urgent, insecure mission; knowing that another soldier was in serious trouble and needed his help. He was sent home before his 365-day tour was over because of his arm wound. Tragically, within only a few months after that night near the DMZ, two of the 6 crews from the 237th Medical Detachment were killed in action. Seven more lives were lost; Don Study being the only one to survive those two helicopter losses. Phil knew that one of them could easily have been him if he had been there for his full tour.

There are 32 names on The Wall for that date, and he took a picture to record them.

Back home in Ohio, he wrote letters to the hometown newspapers of 26 of those names, noting the details of the mission to include the name of "Eddie" in hopes that he might have been a friend. Phil was able to determine through the Vietnam Helicopter Pilots Association that 3 of the names were other helicopter pilots and three of the names were Navy or Marines. He wanted to express his feelings to the family of the soldier that died on that day and let them know that his loss was not entirely in vain. His loss may have allowed others to live.

Several responses to Phil's request were received. Some were hopeful that their son or brother was the one he was looking for and others responded trying to help Phil find answers. After 2 weeks, no more responses were received and Phil was about to give up, not knowing any other avenue to pursue.

In a small town in Wisconsin, Margaret Grotzke was not sure if she should make the phone call or not, but her son encouraged her to do so. Hesitatingly, she dialed the number and was able to tell Phil that Yes, she was the mother of Allen Grotzke, the soldier he was looking for! A long conversation ensued and they became friends, exchanging feelings and mutually supporting each other. After she hung up from the conversation, she remembered that about six months prior, a friend of Allen's had called to talk.

He had been with Allen the day he died and remembering where the Grotzke's were from, he had finally looked up the family. His name was Ed.

Writing a thank you letter to Phil, she gave him the address and phone number of the fellow who called. "Could this be the Eddie that you are looking for?" she wrote. Phil would soon find out.

He called that evening and got Ed's answering machine. Unprepared for a recorder, Phil simply left his name and number and said, "*I* think we have a mutual friend from Vietnam." Two days later, Ed Paradis called from his home in Connecticut, "Is Phil Marshall there? This is Ed Paradis returning his call." Phil acknowledged his question and then asked one of his own, "Were you wounded near the DMZ on 15 November, 1969?" Ed quietly answered, "Yes." Phil continued, "When you were picked up, was the helicopter pilot wounded?" Again, Ed answered, "Yes," but this time not so quietly. Phil smiled to himself and finally told Ed, **"I'm the pilot!"**

Another long conversation and tearful reunion followed as these two "acquaintances" became reacquainted. A little bit of detective work paid off as these two compatriots talked at length of the events of the date that had become so ingrained in their memories. Then, in a moment of silence, Ed sighed and told Phil that he had heard that the rest of his squad of 12 men had been wiped out the next day.

He had not been to the Vietnam Memorial to confirm it and had no way of knowing for certain. Phil offered that he had the picture of the wall with him and could read the names from the following day if Ed would like? Ed's immediate response was, "No" but he thought for a few seconds and then quietly said, "Go ahead..."

As Phil began to read the names, he heard Ed whisper, "No, not him. No, not Smitty, too. No." But it was true; most of his friends had been killed the next day. Had Phil and his crew not risked their lives to save them that night, both Ed and his other buddy would surely have died the next day, too. To this day, they only remember that third wounded soldier as "Sgt. Mueller" and have no idea where he is.

2000 Hours 7 February 1990. Phil Marshall and Ed Paradis sat down with their wives to a steak dinner in Phil's home and talked about family, friends and the events that brought them together. Ed wondered aloud how often a pilot and someone he rescued got together like this? Phil's reply was, "Rarely, Ed; very rarely! In four months I Medevac'd almost 400 guys from the field and unfortunately I have no idea who any of them were except you. They may not know my name or my face, but they know me in their hearts just as I know them in mine." "Besides," Phil continued, "Who would have thought 20 years ago that you and I would some day sit across from each other again and talk about what we have meant to each other?"

The author holding a Shasta Orange soda from the crew of the USS Repose. The Navy Hospital Ship often gave meals and drinks to the Dustoff crews during their long days of flying. Note water wings and M16 slung over the armored seat back.

Author's note: I wrote this in the third person because I did not want to repeatedly use the word "I" and third person was the only way I could think of. In these two short sentences, I have used it 6 times; see what I mean?

Phil

Epilogue:

In April of 2006, I was given the information to contact Larry Mueller in Illinois, the third soldier.

However, two phone calls (the second answered by his wife) went unreturned, so can only surmise he has no desire whatsoever to talk to me... My loss.

WO1 Phil Marshall, 12 November 1969 Red Beach
Aircraft 67-17626

Mission 23

Almost Famous

For the last mission in this book, I wanted to include this one. Over the years, I have met many good people, and one of them was a business associate named Harry J. Kelly, Jr. known by all his friends as simply J-R. A now retired businessman, he earned much respect from all he came in contact with. I had the pleasure of knowing him well enough that he shared the following story with me.

So what is a World War II story doing in a book about flying helicopters in Vietnam? JR's story, to me, is so incredible that I believe it needs to be in print somewhere! I shared JR's mission with a few in the media who thought it interesting, but it has never been published until now. The story is about an ordinary man in extraordinary circumstances, his brush with immortality and a very small snapshot of a leatherneck's exploits in wartime. Here is that story as I wrote it several years ago:

Perhaps the most recognized photo of World War II is the Joe Rosenthal picture of United States Marines raising the flag on Iwo Jima.

So much has been written about those 6 brave men and much is known about their lives. But there is one story that has never been published about that photograph. It took place about 15 feet away...

Harry J. Kelly, Jr., known now by everyone simply as "JR" was a young private with Company F, 2nd Battalion, 28th Regiment, and 5th Marine Division. Company F was the assault company ordered to take Mt. Suribachi with E Company in support. It took them 4 days of fighting to reach an area near the top, and many of JR's comrades did not make it that far, his Company experiencing huge numbers of casualties in their assault up the volcano.

The night before "the photo" was taken, JR and 3 of his buddies found a rocky trench to hunker down in for the night. "The ground was so rocky and very difficult to dig foxholes in. We thought we were very lucky to find this ditch, it sure beat digging." The weather was cold and rainy that night, about 40 degrees he guessed, and they were all soaking wet with only ponchos to protect themselves from the rain. As the night progressed, "we felt our butts getting wet with a trickle of water." That's when they realized that they had taken shelter in a drainage ditch.

They dared not climb out, however, because they were afraid of being shot by the enemy or perhaps even other Marines in the darkness. So they "toughed it out" and by morning, the water was up to their belly buttons!

With the morning light, these 4 soaking ditch dwellers noticed an American flag planted on Mt. Suribachi and they assumed that the objective had been taken. However, as they found out later, someone, apparently from E Company, had placed the flag there and then come back down. Thinking the area was secured; they went about looking for caves to blow up. Then the word came down from his Captain, "F Company has been selected to take Mount Suribachi. We need volunteers to scout ahead." JR noted that at 19, "I was full of pee and vinegar" and became one of four scouts to go ahead of the rest of the group.

The advance up the hill was an "eye opener" for the scouts, as JR was about to observe. Seeing so many Americans on the hill and the scouts closing on their positions, several Japanese blew themselves up with hand grenades rather than be captured. One of the bodies rolled down the hill and stopped at his feet.

Without taking any fire and with no further losses, JR and the other Marines finally secured the hill, blowing up caves in the process to further prevent any "surprises." He remembers finding a Quartermaster supply cache and with the weather from the night before fresh in his mind, he put on a raincoat. "It came up to my elbows."

JR and some others walked to the center of the volcano, and he remarked at how hot the gravel was, so they climbed back out to the rim. Thinking they were going home in the next day or two, they sat on the rock hard ground of the crater rim, looking out at all the ships, picking out the one on which they wanted to go home. "That one looks like it's got the best chow" one exclaimed. "We were happy, giddy and 'BS-ing'" JR recalls. "We had fought hard and survived massive losses; only about 30 of my original company of 250 were still on the hill." They were just simply thrilled to be alive.

"Hey, give me a hand with this pole" someone barked. "Being good Marines, we all 'snapped to'" JR said, thinking it was an officer giving them an order. But like them, it was another private, and he was trying to pull a pole out of a bunker. "You pull your own f***ing pole outta there!" was JR's retort.

"We're takin' a smoke break. Get those guys over there" pointing to another group of Marines. And they got back to picking out ships in the harbor as the private who beckoned them found someone else to help with the pole. Guess which 6 Marines JR pointed to.

"The rest is history" as the saying goes. While Rosenthal was taking the photo of the 6 Marines raising the flag on Iwo, just out of range of the camera lens are 4 Marines, smoking cigarettes, picking out which ship they are going home on. They didn't realize how close they were to immortality.

Later that night, the sky was lit up by what JR estimated to be 600 ships opening fire all at once. "We kept our ponchos over our heads to keep the hot metal off of us." But it was not enough to keep the Japanese from shelling their rudimentary positions on Mt. Suribachi. JR and his buddies survived another night on Iwo Jima and with the dawn, they decided they had had enough with raining water and raining hot steel. They dug what was best described as a pillbox, using big rafters they had scrounged so they could secure a good night's sleep.

They were hardly done with their newly constructed abode when troops from another company of Marines approached. "We'll take this hole" one of them remarked. "You're crazy!" was JR's reply.

But the decision had already been made; Company F was moving out to the north end of the island.

Harry Kelly, Jr., was a citizen of Iwo for a total of 21 days. He stayed there until March 10, 1945, when he was one of the 30 remaining leathernecks out of 250 Company F Marines to hit the beach. While he has always been highly respected by his business associates, he missed being enormously famous by only a very minor set of circumstances. Perhaps no more than a ten foot pole!

Please forward comments or feedback on this book to:

DmzDustoffVietnam@yahoo.com

Autographed/dedicated copies from the author may also be obtained at this address.

All books are available in Braille, Giant Print, Kindle… Auto-delivered wirelessly and for corporate training, premiums, or special promotions.

For details contact:

Charles Lee Emerson
Proprietary Markets
OS Publishing
PO Box 1
Ludlow Falls, Ohio 45339 USA